SpringerBriefs in Educational Communications and Technology

Series Editors

J. Michael Spector, University of North Texas, Denton, TX, USA
M.J. Bishop, University System of Maryland, College Park, MD, USA
Dirk Ifenthaler, University of Mannheim, Mannheim, Germany,
Deakin University, Geelong, Australia

More information about this series at http://www.springernature.com/series/11821

Alexis M. Stoner · Katherine S. Cennamo

Enhancing Reflection within Situated Learning

Incorporating Mindfulness as an Instructional Strategy

 Springer

Alexis M. Stoner
Edward Via College of Osteopathic
Medicine
Carolinas Campus
Spartanburg, SC, USA

Katherine S. Cennamo
School of Education
Virginia Tech School of Education
Blacksburg, VA, USA

ISSN 2196-498X   ISSN 2196-4998   (electronic)
SpringerBriefs in Educational Communications and Technology
ISBN 978-3-319-70325-1   ISBN 978-3-319-70326-8   (eBook)
https://doi.org/10.1007/978-3-319-70326-8

Library of Congress Control Number: 2017962288

© Association for Educational Communications and Technology 2018
This work is subject to copyright. All rights are reserved by the Publisher, whether the whole or part of the material is concerned, specifically the rights of translation, reprinting, reuse of illustrations, recitation, broadcasting, reproduction on microfilms or in any other physical way, and transmission or information storage and retrieval, electronic adaptation, computer software, or by similar or dissimilar methodology now known or hereafter developed.
The use of general descriptive names, registered names, trademarks, service marks, etc. in this publication does not imply, even in the absence of a specific statement, that such names are exempt from the relevant protective laws and regulations and therefore free for general use.
The publisher, the authors and the editors are safe to assume that the advice and information in this book are believed to be true and accurate at the date of publication. Neither the publisher nor the authors or the editors give a warranty, express or implied, with respect to the material contained herein or for any errors or omissions that may have been made. The publisher remains neutral with regard to jurisdictional claims in published maps and institutional affiliations.

Printed on acid-free paper

This Springer imprint is published by Springer Nature
The registered company is Springer International Publishing AG
The registered company address is: Gewerbestrasse 11, 6330 Cham, Switzerland

Preface

It is well accepted that ensuring the ability of learners to transfer acquired knowledge to a variety of situations is key to designing instruction for situated learning. The unpredictable nature of the situated learning environment often makes it difficult for designers to develop instructional strategies that can be applied across learning environments. While reflection has been identified as a key component to situated learning (Brown et al. 1989; Herrington and Oliver 1995), the guidance that exists within the literature to support reflective practice within situated learning primarily focuses on the retroactive reflection-on-action. While reflection-on-action is beneficial, reflection-in-action is thought to enhance learners' ability to meet the demand of the ill-structured nature of authentic learning environments as experienced in situated learning (Schön 1983). One strategy that holds promise for enhancing both forms of reflection is the practice of mindfulness.

The relationship between mindfulness and reflection-in-action has been discussed in contexts such as social work (Mishna and Bogo 2007), medical education (Pezzolesi et al. 2013), organizational management (Jordan et al. 2009), and service-learning (Alrutz and Stewart 2012); however, little attention has been given to this topic within situated learning. Mindfulness is often viewed from a spiritual perspective, aligning with the wisdom traditions (Kabat-Zinn 1982), yet others see mindfulness through a more scientific lens, associated with positive learning outcomes (Ergas 2015). Presented within this monograph, and argued by Ergas (2015) as the intersection between the two perspectives, is incorporating mindfulness as a means of directing attention.

Mindfulness practices will vary based on the instructional environment. However, the premise of this monograph is that it is a metacognitive skill that can be acquired and incorporated into instruction. Arguments within the literature suggest that being mindful within a situated learning environment will help learners increase their attention and focus with less distraction (Bush 2011; Crumley and Schutz 2011; Diaz 2011), enhance their interest and engagement in the experience (Trunnell 1996) and enhance their self-awareness (Birnbaum 2008; Song and Muschert 2014). We propose that incorporating strategies to promote mindfulness may provide learners in a situated learning environment with a heightened awareness to the present moment, which has the potential to enhance their ability to reflect-in-action and, thus, improve their reflective practice.

In order to identify elements essential to integrating mindfulness as an instructional strategy to enhance reflection-in-action within situated learning, a conceptual model was developed using Type 2 design and development research methods for model development and model validation (Richey and Klein 2007). As recommended by Richey and Klein (2007), the research included three key phases: literature review for model development, expert review evaluation for model validation, and revision. The model presented in this monograph brings together the literature on situated learning, reflection-in-action, and mindfulness to derive strategies to improve reflective practice within situated learning by incorporating reflection-in-action and mindfulness. It builds upon Brown et al.'s (1989) instructional model and Herrington and Oliver's (2000) framework for authentic learning environments to ensure that the model is grounded in foundational theoretical roots of situated learning and reflects the evolution of the field and modern recommendations for practice. The model expands on the component of reflection, incorporating it throughout each aspect of situated learning, and identifies the benefits for creating an environment that promotes reflection-in-action. It also illustrates and supports the existing research that mindfulness as an instructional strategy has promise to improve learning outcomes within situated learning and other instructional environments. If learners are able to direct their attention to the present moment by practicing mindfulness, it is more likely that they will be able to engage in the critical thinking processes involved in reflection.

The following chapters provide a foundation for incorporating mindfulness as an instructional strategy to enhance reflection in situated learning. Chapter 1 provides an overview of situated learning and the methods employed to develop the model. Chapters 2, 3, and 4 describe strategies for incorporating reflection in situated learning, reflection-in-action in situated learning, and mindfulness as an instructional strategy in a situated learning environment, respectively. Chapter 5 provides a synthesis of Chaps. 2, 3, and 4 in the creation of a conceptual model of instruction that promotes reflection-in-action by integrating mindfulness for situated learning. Finally, Chap. 6 provides the concluding discussion with implications for future research.

Spartanburg, SC, USA   Alexis M. Stoner
Blacksburg, VA, USA   Katherine S. Cennamo

References

Alrutz, M., & Stewart, T. (2012). Comparison of the effects of reflection and contemplation activities on service-learners' cognitive and affective mindfulness. *McGill Journal of Education, 47*(3), 303–322. https://doi.org/10.7202/1014861ar.

Birnbaum, L. (2008). The use of mindfulness training to create an 'accompanying place' for social work students. *Social Work Education, 27*(8), 837–852. https://doi.org/10.1080/02615470701538330.

Brown, J. S., Collins, A., & Duguid, P. (1989). Situated cognition and the culture of learning. *Educational Researcher, 18*(1), 32–42. https://doi.org/10.2307/1176008.

Bush, M. (2011). Mindfulness in higher education. *Contemporary Buddhism, 12*(1), 183–197. https://doi.org/10.1080/14639947.2011.564838.

Crumley, G., & Schutz, H. (2011). *Short-duration mindfulness training with adult learners* (Vol. 22, pp. 37–42). Bowie: American Association for Adult and Continuing Education.

Diaz, F. M. (2011). Mindfulness, attention, and flow during music listening: An empirical investigation. *Psychology of Music, 41*(1), 42–58. https://doi.org/10.1177/0305735611415144.

Ergas, O. (2015). The Deeper Teachings of Mindfulness-Based 'Interventions' as a Reconstruction of 'Education'. *Journal of Philosophy of Education, 49*(2), 203–220. https://doi.org/10.1111/1467-9752.12137.

Herrington, J., & Oliver, R. (1995). Critical characteristics of situated learning: implications for the instructional design of multimedia.

Herrington, J., & Oliver, R. (2000). An instructional design framework for authentic learning environments. *Educational Technology Research and Development, 48*(3), 23–48. https://doi.org/10.1007/BF02319856.

Jordan, S., Messner, M., & Becker, A. (2009). Reflection and mindfulness in organizations: rationales and possibilities for integration. *MANAGEMENT LEARNING, 40*(4), 465–473. https://doi.org/10.1177/1350507609339687.

Kabat-Zinn, J. (1982). An outpatient program in behavioral medicine for chronic pain patients based on the practice of mindfulness meditation: Theoretical considerations and preliminary results. *General hospital psychiatry, 4*(1), 33–47, https://doi.org/10.1016/0163-8343(82)90026-3.

Mishna, F., & Bogo, M. (2007). Reflective practice in contemporary social work classrooms. *Journal of Social Work Education, 43*(3), 529–544.

Pezzolesi, C., Ghaleb, M., Kostrzewski, A., & Dhillon, S. (2013). Is mindful reflective practice the way forward to reduce medication errors? *International Journal of Pharmacy Practice, 21*(6), 413–416. https://doi.org/10.1111/ijpp.12031.

Richey, R., & Klein, J. D. (2007). Design and development research: methods, strategies, and issues. Mahwah, N.J: L. Erlbaum Associates.

Schön, D. A. (1983). The reflective practitioner: how professionals think in action. New York: Basic Books.

Song, K. Y., & Muschert, G. W. (2014). Opening the Contemplative Mind in the Sociology Classroom. *Humanity & Society, 38*(3), 314–338. https://doi.org/10.1177/0160597614537794.

Trunnell, E. P. (1996). Optimizing an Outdoor Experience for Experiential Learning by Decreasing Boredom through Mindfulness Training. *Journal of Experiential Education, 19*(1), 43.

Contents

About the Authors

Alexis M. Stoner, PhD, MPH is an Assistant Professor of Preventive Medicine and Public Health at the Edward Via College of Osteopathic Medicine. She has a bachelor's degree in Biology from Kenyon College, a master's degree in Public Health from The Ohio State University, and a Ph.D. in Curriculum and Instruction – Instructional Design and Technology from Virginia Tech. During her Ph.D. program, her dissertation explored incorporating mindfulness as an instructional strategy to enhance reflection within a situation learning environment. Currently, her research focuses on incorporating mindfulness within medical education, designing authentic learning experiences for undergraduate medical students, along with developing educational public health initiatives to improve health outcomes among underserved populations. Dr. Stoner has published in various peer-reviewed journals and presented at various conferences in an effort to enhance and further the current literature.

Katherine S. Cennamo, PhD is a Professor of Learning Sciences and Technologies at Virginia Tech. She has a bachelor's degree in Elementary Education from Virginia Tech, a master's degree in Educational Media from the University of Arizona, and a Ph.D. in Instructional Technology from the University of Texas at Austin. Throughout her career, Dr. Cennamo's work has focused on the application of learning theories to the design of technology-based instructional materials. Through numerous funded projects, publications, presentations, instructional materials, and teaching activities, she has disseminated knowledge of instructional strategies based on established theories of learning, illuminated the nature of instructional design practice so that scholars and designers alike better understand their work, and applied this knowledge to the preparation of future instructional design professionals. She has synthesized much of this work in her textbooks, *Real World Instructional Design*, co-authored with Debby Kalk, and *Integrating Technology for Meaningful Classroom Use*, co-authored with John Ross and Peggy Ertmer. Currently, her research and service activities focus on developing and sustaining a classroom culture that fosters critical and creative thinking skills in K-12 and higher education environments.

Chapter 1
Introduction

Many methods of formal education have been criticized for using decontextualized instructional approaches that result in a clear separation between knowing and doing, leaving students with the inability to transfer knowledge (Bransford et al. 1992; Brown et al. 1989). These methods separate the acquisition of knowledge from the context and action in which it is utilized (Resnick 1987). As educational theory evolved, many researchers began to argue that learning and cognition are dependent upon and embedded in the situation (Brown et al. 1989; Herrington and Oliver 2000). As a result, situated learning emerged as a learning theory and a model of instruction that focuses on learning through authentic learning environments in which learners are able to immerse themselves in an academic domain and participate in authentic tasks.

Yet designing instruction for situated learning can be challenging, as authentic environments are often unpredictable and vary greatly across situations and disciplines (Winn 1993). To support situated learners in facing these ill-structured problems and unique environments, it has been suggested that it is essential to develop skills that transfer across environments (Winn 1993). The ability to mindfully reflect-in-action is one such skill. This chapter presents the rationale and methods behind the development of a model to use mindfulness as an instructional strategy to enhance learners' abilities to reflect on their actions within a situated learning environment.

As defined by Collins (1991), "situated learning is the notion of learning knowledge and skills in contexts that reflects the way knowledge will be useful in real life" (p.122). The relationship between the learner and variables in the environment directly impacts the way knowledge is formed and retrieved. According to situated learning theory, knowledge will remain inert if learned outside of the authentic environment in which it is used (Brown et al. 1989). Therefore, the emphasis in situated learning is on placing learners in authentic learning environments that will allow them to acquire the knowledge and skills used in everyday practice (Choi and Hannafin 1995).

© Association for Educational Communications and Technology 2018
A.M. Stoner, K.S. Cennamo, *Enhancing Reflection within Situated Learning*,
SpringerBriefs in Educational Communications and Technology,
https://doi.org/10.1007/978-3-319-70326-8_1

In addition to environmental variables, building on Vygotsky's sociocultural theory, culture is also a key influence in situated learning. Knowledge is built through lived practices within a society; therefore, as Brown et al. (1989) note, knowledge, activity, and culture in which the learning is taking place are intimately connected. The authentic activities in which learners are engaged are simply ordinary practices of the culture (Brown et al. 1989). Learners must understand how to engage with the technologies of the culture, the social practices, and especially the use of language (Lave and Wenger 1991). In situated learning, learners must not only be able to learn from the discourse of the culture but also learn to talk within the culture as an active participant.

In situated learning, learning often occurs through participation within a community of practice. A community of practice is defined as: "an activity system about which participants share understanding concerning what they are doing and what that means in their lives and for their communities" (Lave and Wenger 1991). Learners enter a community of practice as newcomers, and by observing and interacting with the sociocultural aspects of the community, they shape their individual identity and role within the community (Henning 2004). As learners advance in both knowledge and skills, they become full members of the community of practice. According to Lave and Wenger (1991), this process by which a newcomer acquires the knowledge and skills to become a full participant within a community of practice is known as legitimate peripheral participation. It can also be thought of as moving from a beginner to expert status within a practice.

Legitimate peripheral participation describes an invitation into the community of practice that, when supported appropriately, provides access to knowledge and opportunities for involvement and growth inherent in the community. As peripheral participants advance to full participants, they then take on the role of mentoring and teaching the other newcomers in the community of practice. A classic example of legitimate peripheral participation is the apprenticeship. Peripheral participants enter a community of practice as an apprentice observing and learning from the mentorship of a full participant. As they advance in their knowledge and skills, they will begin to take on tasks independently until they have acquired the status of a full participant within the community of practice. Apprenticeship has been used as a form of learning for centuries and is often used today especially in professions that require high pressure and cognitively demanding situations such as the medical field.

Within an authentic learning environment, learners use what Rogoff and Lave (1984) refer to as everyday cognition. This differs from the cognition used in a formal school environment where learners are often required to engage in rote learning in a decontextualized manner (Henning 2004; Lave 1988; Brown et al. 1989). Lave (1988) uses the term "just plain folk" to describe people who use everyday cognition when learning in daily activities. This type of cognition makes use of sociocultural tools and situational clues that aid them in problem-solving when encountering complex problems (Henning 2004). Everyday thinking "is not illogical and sloppy but instead is sensible and effective in handling the practice problem" (Rogoff and Lave 1984). In situated learning, learners engage in everyday problem-solving using the tools and schemas that are socially provided within the environment. Therefore, knowledge is produced from both the activity and cultural implications of situations: the very foundation of situated learning (Brown et al. 1989). While situated learning is used as an instructional strategy across disciplines, it is most commonly implemented through apprenticeships, anchored instruction, placing a learner in an actual work setting such as an internship, or using a simulated or virtual version of an actual work environment (McLellan 1994).

Brown et al. (1989) were the first to propose a model of instruction for situated learning, later followed by the development of a framework which included critical characteristics for the instructional design of authentic learning environments by Herrington and Oliver (2000). This model and framework have provided great insight for instructional designers into effective instructional practices; however for situated learning, the design process can be challenging due to the variability and uncertainty often presented within the learning environment (Winn 1993; Brown and Duguid 1993). In authentic learning environments, learners are presented with ill-structured problems that require enhanced cognitive skills to face and adjust to daily dilemmas (Jonassen 1997; Young 1993); variables and outcomes are unpredictable and rarely consistent across situations. Because of the variability in the experiences of learners who are engaged in situated learning, it is more accurate to think about how designers can design *for* situated learning experiences than to talk about how such learning environments can be designed. The role of the instructional designer is to provide the learner with support to reduce the complexity of the learning environment and to assist the learner in transferring the skills learned in one environment to others (Winn 1993).

The ability to transfer knowledge requires a student to be able to use the knowledge and skills acquired in one situation and apply them to future activities and environments (Winn 1993). Two types of transfer have been identified: low-road transfer and high-road transfer (Salomon and Perkins 1989). Low-road transfer is used when a learner has had extensive practice in the same behavior and the knowledge transfers to a very similar activity in which the learner engages in automaticity in a new context. High-road transfer is more difficult and requires abstraction from one environment for application in a completely different context.

It has been suggested that, especially for high-road transfer, instructional designers should work to develop generic skills that learners can utilize and apply across situations that are not only specific to those in which the learning originally occurred, but adaptable to other situations (Winn 1993). Researchers argue that providing learners with the knowledge and skills to meet the demand of the learning environment will help them adapt to unanticipated difficulties in novel situations (Brown and Duguid 1993).

Reflection to promote abstraction and transfer of knowledge to future situations has been identified in the literature as a key component to situated learning (Brown et al. 1989; Herrington and Oliver 2000). However, there is little discussion within the literature as to how to best incorporate reflection to support learners in a situated learning environment. The role of learners in situated learning differs from that of students in a typical formal learning environment. Learning is embedded in authentic activity, context, and culture, and the learners take on a role of a practitioner. Therefore, reflective learning as suggested by Schön (1983) occurs through reflection-in-action. As reflective practitioners, individuals can think about what they are doing as they are doing it in order to adjust to novel situations and develop effective solutions to ill-structured problems.

However, creating an environment that supports reflective practice can be very difficult. Reflection-in-action requires complex cognitive skills of which most learners and practitioners are not naturally accustomed. Scholars theorize that providing learners with metacognitive strategies to enhance reflection-in-action will allow them to perform better in the moment and find deep meaning when reflecting back on the experience (Horton-Deutsch et al. 2012; Pezzolesi et al. 2013). According to Von Wright (1992), "metacognitive skills refer to the steps that people take to regulate and modify the progress of their cognitive activity: to learn such skills is to acquire procedures which regulate cognitive processes" (p.64). Metacognitive skills do not come naturally to most students and rarely will they spontaneously engage in metacognitive thinking (Lin 2001). Therefore, when designing instructional environments, especially those of situated learning, Lin (2001) stresses the importance of including metacognitive support to enhance learning.

One metacognitive skill that has been illustrated and suggested to enhance reflection-in-action is mindfulness (Nugent et al. 2011; Mishna and Bogo 2007; Jordan et al. 2009; Epstein 1999). A commonly accepted definition of mindfulness includes one's awareness and attention to the present moment and accepting the experience in a nonjudgmental way (Baer et al. 2004; Bush 2011; Davis 2014; Kabat-Zinn 1982). Researchers have theorized that within the situated learning environment, learners who engage in mindfulness could have the ability to free themselves of preconceived perceptions and the reliance on tacit knowledge, allowing them to more effectively engage reflection-in-action which will aid in problem-solving and transfer of knowledge (Horton-Deutsch et al. 2012). While the relationship between mindfulness and reflection-in-action has been discussed in contexts such as social work (Mishna and Bogo 2007), medical education (Pezzolesi et al. 2013), organizational management (Jordan et al. 2009), and service-learning (Alrutz and Stewart 2012), little attention has been given to this topic within situated learning.

The premise of this monograph is that reflection-in-action and mindfulness are essential skills for practitioners that can be translated across instructional environments. We present a conceptual model that describes effective strategies to enhance reflective practices within situated learning by integrating mindfulness strategies to promote reflection-in-action. By integrating activities to facilitate mindfulness, instructional designers could address some of the challenges faced when designing for situated learning, particularly in promoting reflection within the environment, by enhancing reflection-in-action.

A comprehensive literature review was the foundation for the model. Through comparison methods, the literature was analyzed to identify patterns and overlap between the key concepts and strategies of mindfulness and reflection-in-action as applicable within situated learning, with the intent of providing recommendations and best practices of each variable grounded in data within the literature. Literature was reviewed within the field of situated learning but also spanned other educational disciplines that are similar or applicable to practices of situated learning. Studies examining reflection were limited to only situated learning environments. Studies of reflection-in-action were limited to those within situated and experiential learning environments, as well as within the practice of a reflective practitioner. Studies of mindfulness were limited to those that examined mindfulness from an educational perspective. After applying the exclusion criteria to the literature search, a total of 33 empirical studies were identified and used as data for the development of the model. Of the total articles, 13 focused on strategies for promoting reflection within situated learning, 8 on strategies for reflection-in-action within situated learning, and 12 on strategies for mindfulness within education.

Validity and dependability are critical for the model to be a successful addition to the field of instructional design and situated learning. In order to determine if the model developed was accurate and appropriately supports enhanced reflection-in-action for situated learning, as well as appropriately defines and illustrates the relationship between all variables, three expert reviewers were recruited to review and analyze the model. The experts were recruited from the following areas of expertise for proper triangulation: situated learning, mindfulness, and reflection. Based on their expert opinions, the reviewers evaluated if the model appropriately supports incorporating mindfulness to enhance reflection-in-action in a situated learning environment. As this was a process of formative evaluation, in the final phase of the research, the model was revised to incorporate the expert reviewers' recommendations and revisions. Data collected using the results from the reviews was analyzed individually and then synthesized to modify and improve the model developed in this research.

The following chapters provide a foundation for incorporating mindfulness as an instructional strategy to enhance reflection in situated learning. Chapters 2, 3, and 4 describe strategies for incorporating reflection in situated learning, reflection-in-action in situated learning, and mindfulness as an instructional strategy in a situated learning environment, respectively. Each chapter first presents a brief discussion of the key concepts of the chapter, and then a summary of strategies that empirical literature suggests will enhance that process. Chapter 5 provides a synthesis of Chaps. 2, 3, and 4 through the presentation of a conceptual model of instruction that promotes reflection-in-action by integrating mindfulness for situated learning. Finally, Chap. 6 provides the concluding discussion with implications for future research.

References

Alrutz, M., & Stewart, T. (2012). Comparison of the effects of reflection and contemplation activities on service-learners' cognitive and affective mindfulness. *McGill Journal of Education, 47*(3), 303–322. https://doi.org/10.7202/1014861ar.

Baer, R. A., Smith, G. T., & Allen, K. B. (2004). Assessment of mindfulness by self-report: The Kentucky inventory of mindfulness skills. *Assessment, 11*(3), 191–206. https://doi.org/10.1177/1073191104268029.

Bransford, J. D., Sherwood, R. D., Hasselbring, T. S., Kinzer, C. K., & Williams, S. M. (1992). Anchored instruction: Why we need it and how technology can help. In D. Nix & R. Spiro (Eds.), *Cognition, education, and multimedia* (pp. 115–141). Hillsdale: Erlbaum.

Brown, J. S., & Duguid, P. (1993). Stolen knowledge. *Educational Technology, 33*(3), 10.

Brown, J. S., Collins, A., & Duguid, P. (1989). Situated cognition and the culture of learning. *Educational Researcher, 18*(1), 32–42. https://doi.org/10.2307/1176008.

Bush, M. (2011). Mindfulness in higher education. *Contemporary Buddhism, 12*(1), 183–197. https://doi.org/10.1080/14639947.2011.564838.

Choi, J.-I., & Hannafin, M. (1995). Situated cognition and learning environments: Roles, structures, and implications for design. *Educational Technology Research and Development, 43*(2), 53–69. https://doi.org/10.1007/BF02300472.

Collins, A. (1991). Cognitive apprenticeship and instructional technology. In L. Idol & B. F. Jones (Eds.), *Educational values and cognitive instruction: Implications for reform* (pp. 119–136). Hillsdale: Lawrence Erlbaugm Associates.

Davis, D. J. (2014). *Mindfulness in teaching, learning, and leadership: Implications for higher education.* Paper presented at the The Clute Institute International Academic Conference, Orlando.

Epstein, R. M. (1999). Mindful practice. *JAMA, 282*(9), 833–839. https://doi.org/10.1001/jama.282.9.833.

Henning, P. H. (2004). Everyday cognition and situated learning. In D. H. Jonassen (Ed.), *Handbook of research on educational communications and technology* (2nd ed.). Mahwah: Lawrence Erlbaum.

Herrington, J., & Oliver, R. (2000). An instructional design framework for authentic learning environments. *Educational Technology Research and Development, 48*(3), 23–48. https://doi.org/10.1007/BF02319856.

Horton-Deutsch, S., Drew, B. L., & Beck-Coon, K. (2012). Mindful learners. In *Reflective practice transforming education and improving outcomes* (pp. 79–96). Indianapolis: Sigma Theta Tau International Honor Society of Nursing.

Jonassen, D. H. (1997). Instructional design models for well-structured and ill-structured problem-solving learning outcomes. *Educational Technology Research and Development, 45*(1), 65–94.

Jordan, S., Messner, M., & Becker, A. (2009). Reflection and mindfulness in organizations: Rationales and possibilities for integration. *Management Learning, 40*(4), 465–473. https://doi.org/10.1177/1350507609339687.

Kabat-Zinn, J. (1982). An outpatient program in behavioral medicine for chronic pain patients based on the practice of mindfulness meditation: Theoretical considerations and preliminary results. *General Hospital Psychiatry, 4*(1), 33–47. https://doi.org/10.1016/0163-8343(82)90026-3.

Lave, J. (1988). *Cognition in practice: Mind, mathematics, and culture in everyday life* (Vol. Book, Whole). Cambridge/New York: Cambridge University Press.

Lave, J., & Wenger, E. (1991). *Situated learning: Legitimate peripheral participation* (Vol. Book, Whole). New York: Cambridge University Press.

Lin, X. (2001). Designing metacognitive activities. *Educational Technology Research and Development, 49*(2), 23–40. https://doi.org/10.1007/BF02504926.

McLellan, H. (1994). Situated learning: Continuing the conversation. *Educational Technology, 34*(8), 7.

Mishna, F., & Bogo, M. (2007). Reflective practice in contemporary social work classrooms. *Journal of Social Work Education, 43*(3), 529–544.

Nugent, P., Moss, D., Barnes, R., & Wilks, J. (2011). Clear (ing) space: Mindfulness-based reflective practice. *Reflective Practice, 12*(1), 1–13.

Pezzolesi, C., Ghaleb, M., Kostrzewski, A., & Dhillon, S. (2013). Is mindful reflective practice the way forward to reduce medication errors? *International Journal of Pharmacy Practice, 21*(6), 413–416. https://doi.org/10.1111/ijpp.12031.

Resnick, L. B. (1987). The 1987 presidential address learning in school and out. *Educational Researcher, 16*(9), 13–54. https://doi.org/10.3102/0013189X016009013.

Rogoff, B. E., & Lave, J. E. (1984). *Everyday cognition: Its development in social context.* Cambridge, MA, Harvard University press.

Salomon, G., & Perkins, D. N. (1989). Rocky roads to transfer: Rethinking mechanism of a neglected phenomenon. *Educational Psychologist, 24*(2), 113–142.

Schön, D. A. (1983). *The reflective practitioner: How professionals think in action* (Vol. Book, Whole). New York: Basic Books.

Von Wright, J. (1992). Reflections on reflection. *Learning and Instruction, 2*(1), 59–68. https://doi.org/10.1016/0959-4752(92)90005-7.

Winn, W. (1993). Instructional design and situated learning: Paradox or partnership? *Educational Technology, 33*(3), 16.

Young, M. F. (1993). Instructional design for situated learning. *Educational Technology Research and Development, 41*(1), 43–58. https://doi.org/10.1007/BF02297091.

Chapter 2
Strategies for Reflection in Situated Learning

2.1 Reflection in Situated Learning

Common to both Brown et al.'s (1989) model of instruction and Herrington and Oliver's (2000) framework, along with other experiential learning models, is the importance of including activities for promoting reflection within the design of the learning environment. It is assumed that, through reflection, students can form abstract conceptualizations that will aid in both low-road and high-road transfer. As described by Norman (2014), reflection is necessary for cognitive restructuring and the ability to criticize tacit performance. Evidence suggests that it also provides many learning benefits, allowing the learners to critically analyze their performance, make comparisons between themselves and other students and experts within the environment, and understand how learning can apply to future situations (Collins 1991). Based on their research in anchored instruction, the Cognition and Technology Group at Vanderbilt (1990) purposes that providing opportunities for reflection within situated learning has the greatest potential to help learners transfer knowledge and further research is needed on this topic to aid in the instructional design process (CTGV 1990).

Reflective learning comes in many forms and is executed differently in various instructional settings. It often occurs through both individual and social interaction, allowing learners to develop new perspectives and understanding of their own learning (Collins 1991; Lin et al. 1999). In situated learning, learners develop knowledge and skills through their experiences and their interaction with the community and environment. The value of reflection when learning through experience was first discussed by John Dewey and, later, further expanded by David Kolb and other researchers who focused on the importance of reflection within experiential learning. Dewey (1938) believed reflection is necessary in order to connect experience and theory, as new knowledge is created when learners move between experience and reflection. It has been suggested that when students reflect on their experiences

© Association for Educational Communications and Technology 2018
A.M. Stoner, K.S. Cennamo, *Enhancing Reflection within Situated Learning*,
SpringerBriefs in Educational Communications and Technology,
https://doi.org/10.1007/978-3-319-70326-8_2

Table 2.1 Strategies for promoting reflection in situated learning

Strategies	Methods to support incorporating the strategy
1. Build a context and environment that promotes reflection (Granville and Dison 2005; Ovens and Tinning 2009; Huisman and Edwards 2011)	• Include context that provides a relatable experience for students (Granville and Dison 2005; Huisman and Edwards 2011) • Utilize an authentic context and environment (Croker et al. 1998; Herrington and Oliver 2000; Herrington et al. 2014)
2. Incorporate social interaction with others (Herrington and Oliver 2000; Bell and Mladenovic 2015; Eick et al. 2003)	• Create opportunities for collaborative group work (Herrington and Oliver 2000) • Peer observation (Bell and Mladenovic 2015) • Provide opportunities for observation and interaction with experts (Herrington and Oliver 2000; Eick et al. 2003; Croker et al. 1998)
3. Consider duration and timing (Boudreau et al. 2014; Bringle and Hatcher 1999; Carroll 2009; Eyler 2001, 2002; Granville and Dison 2005; Huisman and Edwards 2011; Stalmeijer et al. 2009; Stewart 2010)	• Consider a longer duration of learning experience (Boudreau et al. 2014; Granville and Dison 2005; Huisman and Edwards 2011; Stalmeijer et al. 2009) • Include opportunities for reflection early on: Reflection-before-action (Bringle and Hatcher 1999; Carroll 2009; Eyler 2001, 2002; Granville and Dison 2005; Stewart 2010)
4. Provide feedback (Stalmeijer et al. 2009; Herrington and Oliver 2000; Herrington et al. 2014)	• Use a variety of sources: Feedback from experts, instructors, and other students (Stalmeijer et al. 2009; Herrington and Oliver 2000; Herrington et al. 2014)
5. Provide opportunities to revisit an experience (Croker et al. 1998; Herrington and Oliver 2000; Stalmeijer et al. 2009)	• Nonlinear navigation (Croker et al. 1998) • Include self-observation (Stalmeijer et al. 2009)
6. Promote spontaneous reflection (Boudreau et al. 2014; Herrington et al. 2014)	• Develop reflection skills of the learners (Boudreau et al. 2014; Herrington et al. 2014)

in situated learning, they enhance their ability to transfer knowledge to other environments (CTGV 1990). Additional benefits of reflecting during situated learning that have been found in the literature include opportunities for the learners to analyze their performance and determine how to improve in future experience, compare themselves to experts and other practitioners in assessing essential knowledge and skills for improved outcomes, characterize strategies, and compare multiple performances to form abstractions (Collins 1991).

Currently, there is little guidance within the literature on how to design for reflection within a situated learning environment. However, there are strategies described within the literature, which, when included in situated learning, have been found to promote reflection. These strategies, along with methods to support incorporating these strategies, are illustrated in Table 2.1 and include building a context and environment that promotes reflection, incorporating social interaction, considering duration and timing of reflection, providing feedback, providing nonlinear navigation, and promoting spontaneous reflection. Each of these will be elaborated in the paragraphs that follow.

2.2 Build a Context and Environment that Promotes Reflection

Situated learning provides an opportunity for authentic learning to occur in a variety of settings and includes many different types of activities. Within the empirical evidence, it is apparent that context and the environment directly impact both the type and quality of reflection (Granville and Dison 2005). When the context enables students to form a connection and feel invested with the experience, students have been found to have a better quality and level of reflection (Granville and Dison 2005). Within their study on student teacher reflection practices in a situated learning experience, Ovens and Tinning (2009) found learners use different types of reflection within different contexts and "the discursive nature of each setting mediates the forms of activity, consciousness, and reflection that occurs in that setting" (p.1130). Additional research found when designed correctly, the context of the learning environment will help the students see the value in the learning experience, allowing them to connect and engage in more meaningful reflection (Huisman and Edwards 2011).

Key to helping students make these connections is creating or utilizing an authentic context and environment. Croker et al. (1998) conducted a study utilizing a situated learning framework to design an interactive multimedia program for nurses learning medication administration skills. They found that in order for students to reflect meaningfully on their learning, the program needed to provide authentic contexts and tasks with which students could readily identify. Authentic contexts have been found in other studies to promote reflection as they are associated with helping learners spontaneously reflect without the use of external cues or forced reflection exercises (Herrington and Oliver 2000; Herrington et al. 2014).

2.3 Incorporate Social Interaction with Others

While reflection can often be an individualized experience, within situated learning, social interaction has been found to enhance students' reflective processes. When students were placed in collaborative groups, reflection was naturally encouraged as "the students frequently returned to the experience recollecting the important considerations and relating them to their partners" (Herrington and Oliver 2000, p. 39). One form of social interaction in situated learning that promotes reflective practice is peer observation. Through peer observation, students are likely to engage in reflection as it allows them to critically think about their own practices in context and compare themselves to the practices of others (Bell and Mladenovic 2015). For example, in Bell and Mladenovic's (2015) study on the impact of peer observation for tutor development in a situated learning environment, the students reported, "It is great because the person you are reviewing is teaching the same content, so you can see how different tutors interact/engage with study. You can see/understand what you do well/poorly and what the person you are reviewing does well/poorly" (p. 28). In addition, based on an extensive review of the literature, it was suggested that the opportunity to observe and interact with experts within the context of practice promotes and enhances reflection (Herrington and Oliver 2000). Experts' performance provides a benchmark for which the learners can compare themselves as they engage in reflection (Croker et al. 1998). By reflecting on experts' performances, students have been found to learn how to make adjustments within the context of the authentic activity (Eick et al. 2003).

2.4 Provide Feedback

As with most instructional designs, feedback appears to play a role in promoting reflection in a situated learning environment. In focus group interviews of undergraduate medical students involved in clerkships, students reported their reflection was greatly supported through multisource feedback (Stalmeijer et al. 2009). Specifically, when students received feedback from experts or instructors identifying their strengths and weaknesses, they found value in the reflective experience. Incorporating opportunities for feedback into the design of situated learning experiences has been found to help students reevaluate the experience and understand how to integrate new knowledge for future use (Herrington and Oliver 2000). Additionally, as situated learning can often be a new and variable environment for the student, feedback has been shown to provide the student support and reinforcement to help him or her reach further academically through reflection (Herrington et al. 2014).

2.5 Consider Duration and Timing

There is evidence in the literature that supports consideration of timing in promoting reflection within situated learning. When situated learning experiences are longer in duration, students have been found to engage in more regular reflection (Huisman and Edwards 2011; Stalmeijer et al. 2009). Also, in learning experiences of longer duration, researchers found students are more engaged and involved in the experiences, allowing them to feel more invested, and as a result, they reflected more meaningfully (Granville and Dison 2005). Another study indicated that reflection becomes more of a natural habit, with students reflecting spontaneously the longer they participate in a situated learning experience (Boudreau, Macdonald, & Steinert 2014).

In addition to a longer learning experience, reflection in situated learning is promoted when it is encouraged and incorporated very early on in the learning process. This helps build a habitual foundation from which learners will engage in deeper reflection more frequently throughout a learning experience (Granville and Dison 2005). Encouraging reflection early on in experiential learning often involves engaging in reflection prior to the experience. Building an environment and relationships that facilitate reflection will aid the students in engaging in reflection prior to entering an authentic learning experience (Carroll 2009). Creating an atmosphere of trust between the instructor and students is important to ensure students are open to questioning themselves and others (Bringle and Hatcher 1999). Helping students become aware of their own personal perceptions, assumptions, and feelings about the learning experience is important to raise self-awareness (Eyler 2001, 2002). Reflection-before-action allows them to confront their personal beliefs and sets the foundation for continual self-monitoring and observant behavior during the learning experience (Eyler 2002; Stewart 2010).

2.6 Provide Opportunities to Revisit an Experience

Another strategy that has been shown to promote reflection within situated learning is nonlinear navigation or the opportunity to return to a previous section of the learning experience. This feature is possible mainly in a computer-mediated learning activity. However, by allowing students to return to experiences, reflection is facilitated (Croker et al. 1998), and students can reevaluate the experience while attending to their feelings (Herrington and Oliver 2000). Another method for nonlinear navigation that facilitates reflection is through self-observation. For example, in a clinical setting using cognitive apprenticeships, students were videotaped and later had the opportunity to watch themselves and discuss the performance. This strategy not only facilitated reflection but also helped students understand the value in self-reflection (Stalmeijer et al. 2009).

2.7 Promoting Spontaneous Reflection

Situated learning environments are intended to be authentic ones in which learners are actively engaged in the activity. Therefore, as determined in a study on outcomes of a physician apprenticeship course, it is important for learners to develop the skills to reflect spontaneously as reflection will need to occur as a result of surprises and unfamiliar events (Boudreau 2014). The authenticity of the environment is lessened when moments are taken to try and teach learners how to intentionally reflect. However, if given the skills, it is likely they will develop the ability to spontaneously reflect within the situation independently. It is argued, "The provision of the conditions conducive to reflection-rather than explicit direction-provide a powerful enabler for this most critical of learning functions" (Herrington et al. 2014, p. 9). Strategies that have been found in the literature to help learners reflect spontaneously include engaging in authentic tasks and including opportunities for reflection-on-action to further enhance the reflective process (Herrington et al. 2014).

References

Bell, A., & Mladenovic, R. (2015). Situated learning, reflective practice and conceptual expansion: Effective peer observation for tutor development. *Teaching in Higher Education, 20*(1), 24–36. https://doi.org/10.1080/13562517.2014.945163.

Boudreau, J. D., Macdonald, M. E., & Steinert, Y. (2014). Affirming professional identities through an apprenticeship: Insights from a four-year longitudinal case study. *Academic Medicine, 89*(7), 1038–1045. https://doi.org/10.1097/ACM.0000000000000293.

Bringle, R. G., & Hatcher, J. A. (1999). Reflection in service learning: Making meaning of experience. *Educational Horizons, 77*(4), 179.

Brown, J. S., Collins, A., & Duguid, P. (1989). Situated cognition and the culture of learning. *Educational Researcher, 18*(1), 32–42. doi:10.2307/1176008.

Carroll, M. (2009). From mindless to mindful practice: On learning reflection in supervision. *Psychotherapy in Australia, 15*(4), 38.

Collins, A. (1991). Cognitive apprenticeship and instructional technology. In L. Idol & B. F. Jones (Eds.), *Educational values and cognitive instruction: Implications for reform* (pp. 119–136). Hillsdale: Lawrence Erlbaugm Associates.

Croker, F., Alison, J., Stillman, G., White, B., & Tonkin, C. (1998). Situated learning as a model for the design of an interactive multimedia program on medication administration for nurses. *Innovations in Education & Training International, 35*(4), 329–336. https://doi.org/10.1080/1355800980350408.

Dewey, J. (1938). *Experience and education.* New York: Macmillan.

Eick, C. J., Ware, F. N., & Williams, P. G. (2003). Coteaching in a science methods course: A situated learning model of becoming a teacher. *Journal of Teacher Education, 54*(1), 74–85. https://doi.org/10.1177/0022487102238659.

Eyler, J. (2001). Creating your reflection map. *New Directions for Higher Education, 2001*(114), 35–43. https://doi.org/10.1002/he.11.

Eyler, J. (2002). Reflection: Linking service and learning – linking students and communities. *The Journal of Social Issues, 58*(3), 517.

Granville, S., & Dison, L. (2005). Thinking about thinking: Integrating self-reflection into an academic literacy course. *Journal of English for Academic Purposes, 4*(2), 99–118. https://doi.org/10.1016/j.jeap.2004.07.009.

Herrington, J., & Oliver, R. (2000). An instructional design framework for authentic learning environments. *Educational Technology Research and Development, 48*(3), 23–48. https://doi.org/10.1007/BF02319856.

Herrington, J., Parker, J., & Boase-Jelinek, D. (2014). Connected authentic learning: Reflection and intentional learning. *Australian Journal of Education, 58*(1), 23–35. https://doi.org/10.1177/0004944113517830.

Huisman, S., & Edwards, A. (2011). Experiential learning: An exploration of situated and service learning. *AILACTE Journal, 8*, 15.

Lin, X., Hmelo, C., Kinzer, C. K., & Secules, T. J. (1999). Designing technology to support reflection. *Educational Technology Research and Development, 47*(3), 43–62. https://doi.org/10.1007/BF02299633.

Norman, D. (2014). *Things that make us smart: Defending human attributes in the age of the machine* (Vol. Book, Whole). New York: Diversion Books.

Ovens, A., & Tinning, R. (2009). Reflection as situated practice: A memory-work study of lived experience in teacher education. *Teaching and Teacher Education, 25*(8), 1125–1131. https://doi.org/10.1016/j.tate.2009.03.013.

Stalmeijer, R. E., Dolmans, D., Wolfhagen, I., & Scherpbier, A. (2009). Cognitive apprenticeship in clinical practice: Can it stimulate learning in the opinion of students? *Advances in Health Sciences Education, 14*(4), 535–546. https://doi.org/10.1007/s10459-008-9136-0.

Stewart, T. (2010). Opening up service-learning reflection by turning inward: Developing mindful learneres through contemplation. In *Problematizing service-learning critical reflections for development and action* (pp. 37–70). Charlotte: Information Age Publishing.

The Cognition and Technology Group at Vanderbilt, (CTVG), (1990). Anchored instruction and its relationship to situated cognition. *Educational Researcher, 19*(6), 2–10. https://doi.org/10. 3102/0013189X019006002.

Chapter 3
Strategies for Reflection-in-Action in Situated Learning

3.1 Reflection-in-Action in Situated Learning

Most of the current recommendations for supporting reflection in situated learning focus on reflecting after the experience or what Schön (1983) describes as reflection-on-action. However, in situated learning, learners not only fill the role of students, but they become practitioners within an authentic environment. As a practitioner, as stressed and described by Schön (1983), it is not enough to engage only in reflection-on-action. It has been proposed that, in order to prepare learners to face novel situations and deal with the ill-structured problems situated learning presents, they need to develop self-awareness and learn how to reason within a given situation (Winn 1993). Situated learners could benefit and improve performance by increasing their capability to be adaptive thinkers with the ability to solve problems and reflect within the present moment of the experience. This type of practice, according to Schön (1983), is referred to as reflection-in-action.

Whether it is practitioners in the workforce or students in a typical classroom, people engage in regular tacit actions every day, resulting in automated behavior, outside of their conscious awareness. Behavior and performance are carried out with little to no thought prior to engaging in the action. This, according to Schön (1983), is known as knowing-in-action. Within a community of practice, the full members of participation have the greatest level of knowing-in-action as they likely engage in practice without thinking about how they learned the material or their personal recognitions, judgments, and actions prior to performance. However, when confronted with a "surprise" or a moment of unique uncertainty, knowing-in-action can often leave learners and practitioners without a proper response to adjust to the situation. A reflective practitioner, on the other hand, when facing surprises in the environment, either good or undesirable, will respond by engaging in reflection-in-action or thinking about an action while in the midst of performance. Reflection-in-action allows one to analyze and criticize tacit performance and think about feelings,

© Association for Educational Communications and Technology 2018
A.M. Stoner, K.S. Cennamo, *Enhancing Reflection within Situated Learning*, SpringerBriefs in Educational Communications and Technology, https://doi.org/10.1007/978-3-319-70326-8_3

perceptions, and actions as they are occurring in order to better adjust to the present moment and perform optimally. When facing unfamiliar environments with uncertainty and ill-structured problems similar to those of situated learning environments, reflection-in-action could be an effective tool in adapting to the situation and determining an effective solution.

Reflection-in-action strategies are incorporated in many learning environments and have been shown to increase reflective practice such as reflection-on-action, overall performance (Jordan et al. 2009), and the ability to engage in critical thinking skills (Austin et al. 2008). As described by Horton-Deutsch et al. (2012):

> Reflection-in-action is a complex cognitive activity that requires learners to be conscious of what they are doing and how they are doing it in the moment of practice. Processes for reflecting-in-action are those creative strategies that learners can use in the moment of practice, when learners are being, thinking, and doing simultaneously. (p.80).

Contrasting with reflection-in-action, and most often utilized in situated learning and other educational environments, is reflection-on-action. Reflection-on-action occurs when learners reflect after the experience, resulting in no connection to the present moment (Schön 1983). Typically, reflection-on-action allows for greater length of reflective time and a more intensive state of reflection (Carroll 2009). This permits one to engage in personal curiosity and inquiry to understand the individual perspective, behavior, and future implications of the past experience on which the reflection is occurring (Carroll 2009; Schön 1983). Practitioners, who learn to effectively reflect-in-action and critically reflect-on-action, have the ability to improve their tacit knowledge and further improve everyday performance (Schön 1983).

Situated learners act as practitioners as part of the learning environment and in some types of situated learning become members of a community of practice. Becoming reflective practitioners will assist them in facing conflict and uncertainty in novel situations. While reflection-in-action is a fundamental component of becoming a reflective practitioner, the literature on methods for reflection in situated learning has primarily focused on reflection-on-action. In order to understand how mindfulness can support reflection-in-action during situated learning, it is important to understand strategies to promote reflection-in-action within situated learning or similar learning environments. As illustrated in Table 3.1 and discussed below, several strategies are apparent within the literature that should be included in the design for reflection-in-action during situated learning environments: build a context and environment that promotes reflection-in-action, incorporate social interaction with others, develop learners' level of personal awareness, incorporate multiple forms of reflection, and incorporate feedback throughout the experience. Many of these strategies overlap with the general strategies for reflection described in Chap. 2; however, methods to support incorporating these strategies differ in regard to promoting learners' reflection-in-action. Within a model for reflection in situated learning, these strategies can be combined in order to help students learn to become reflective before, during, and after a learning experience.

Table 3.1 Strategies for reflection-in-action in situated learning

Strategies	Methods to support incorporating the strategy
1. Build a context and environment that promotes reflection-in-action (Jordan 2010; Seibert 1999; Edwards 2010)	• Expose learners to a variety of practices within an experience (Jordan 2010) • Create an authentic context and environment (Edwards 2010) • Provide a comfortable and open-minded environment (Edwards 2010; Seibert 1999) • Include promotive and directive pressure (Russell et al. 2011; Seibert 1999)
2. Incorporate social interaction with others (Russell et al. 2011; Seibert 1999; Edwards 2010)	• Provide opportunities for engagement and observing of peers (Russell et al. 2011; Seibert 1999; Edwards 2010) • Provide opportunities for engagement of experts (Russell et al. 2011)
3. Develop learners' level of personal awareness (Mishna and Bogo 2007)	• Develop learners' level of self-awareness (Mishna and Bogo 2007) • Develop learners' level of awareness of the environment and surroundings (Mishna and Bogo 2007)
4. Incorporate multiple forms of reflection (Seibert 1999; Keevers and Treleaven 2011; Goh 2012; Russell et al. 2011)	• Reflection-on-action (Seibert 1999) • Include multiple opportunities for reflection (Seibert 1999; Keevers and Treleaven 2011; Goh 2012; Russell et al. 2011) • Incorporate mindfulness to enhance reflection (Goh 2012; Russell et al. 2011)
5. Provide feedback (Jordan 2010; Seibert 1999)	• Incorporate feedback from learners' personal reflection (Seibert 1999) • Incorporate feedback from learners' performance results (Seibert 1999) • Include critique from experts and peers (Jordan 2010; Seibert 1999)

3.2 Build a Context and Environment that Promotes Reflection-in-Action

As described in Chap. 1, learners often have difficulty facing new situations due to their natural ability to engage in automated behavior as a result of their knowing-in-action (Schön 1983). It has been found that exposing learners to a variety of experiences will help introduce learners to reflection-in-action and is linked with an increase in reflective practice within the experience (Jordan 2010). Jordan (2010) assessed several different practices in order to determine how to best support novice nurses in becoming reflective practitioners within the anesthesiology setting. Utilizing "on the-job training, interdisciplinary case-based teaching, systematic emphasis on the genesis of practices through 'war stories', and monthly rotation through the sub-departments" (Jordan 2010, p. 408), the authors found the diverse practices incorporated were linked to more reflective practitioners.

Another important variable associated with context and the learning environment is the creation of an authentic environment in which learners feel comfortable engaging in reflection. This must occur from the beginning of the experience in order for learners to develop skills to become reflective practitioners. Specifically, Edwards (2010) found Library and Information Services undergraduate students were more likely to engage in reflection-in-action when they felt there was an openness within the environment to speak up and ask questions without feeling embarrassed or uncertain. Additionally, feeling independent and taking ownership in their learning and performance within the environment have been associated with learners thinking for themselves (Seibert 1999). Therefore, integrating a level of autonomy for learners was recommended as a condition conducive for reflection-in-action. Reflection-in-action is also supported when learners are situated within an authentic learning environment. Learners are more reflective when they are interacting with situations and materials in which they are able to personally connect and feel relevant (Edwards 2010).

A final environmental condition conducive for reflection-in-action was identified by Seibert (1999). Through case study research using qualitative interviews, the researchers determined that including a level of promotive and directive pressure helped the learners engage in reflection-in-action. Within Seibert's (1999) study, pressure included time demands and exposure to large amounts of new information. Learners were able to reflect-in-action, meeting the demands of the situation, and were also able to see the products of their performance which was another important component for reflection-in-action as further described below.

3.3   Incorporate Social Interaction with Others

Within situated learning and organizational practice, reflection-in-action becomes very much a social process (Jordan 2010); thus, when designing for a situated learning environment, opportunities for social interaction should be incorporated. Within a social context, a reflective practitioner develops interactive methods to approach novel situations through engaging with others. As argued in the literature, by engaging and observing not only peers but also skilled and knowledgeable individuals, learners are provided with new ideas and perspectives that promote reflection-in-action and adaption to a situation (Russell et al. 2011; Seibert 1999). For example, Edwards (2010) found students reported group work enhanced reflection-in-action: "Working in groups to actually apply the things we have learned is very helpful because we can see how they can be used and get help and new ideas from classmates" (p.22). Social work teachers engaging in reflection-in-action also self-reported, through reflective journals and intergroup dialogue, that their students learned how to become more reflective by observing them which created an environment for learners to practice reflection-in-action (Russell et al. 2011).

3.4   Develop Learners' Level of Personal Awareness

In order for learners to engage in reflection-in-action, they need to not only develop a strong personal awareness but also an awareness of the environment and their surroundings (Mishna and Bogo 2007). In their study on the reflective practitioner paradigm for social work instructors facing conflict in the classroom, Mishna and Bogo (2007) found a sound understanding of one's personal thoughts and feelings, along with the ability to appropriately respond to a situation, will directly impact a practitioner's ability to engage in reflection-in-action. Also, within a situated learning environment, there are many outside cues, dynamics, and variables a learner must learn to attend to or decide to ignore. An awareness of the environment and how to accept or reject these variables has been illustrated by Mishna and Bogo (2007) to aid a learner in engaging in reflection-in-action.

3.5   Incorporate Multiple Forms of Reflection

Reflection-in-action is supported when learners have multiple opportunities and engage in multiple forms of reflection. This is similar to one of Eyler and Giles' 5Cs of critical reflection: continuity (Eyler and Giles 1999). This concept illustrates that learners should be engaging in reflection before, during, and after the experience as all three phases of reflection support and enhance one another. Within situated learning, Seibert's (1999) research has listed reflection-on-action as one of their five conditions for reflection-in-action. Within the study, they recommend learners taking moments in solitude to engage in processing new information and the experiences in which they were previously engaged. A practice-based study also found "multiple forms of reflection can strengthen and co-shape one another" (p.505) helping learners engage not only in routine activities but also when encountering surprises (Keevers and Treleaven 2011). As part of including multiple forms of reflection, integrating mindfulness throughout the experience enhances reflection-in-action (Goh 2012; Mishna and Bogo 2007; Russell et al. 2011). Coupled with mindfulness, research has shown engaging in multiple forms of reflection enables learners to observe and process thoughts, feelings, and behaviors to become reflective practitioners and improve performance (Goh 2012; Russell et al. 2011). Putting the pieces together will encourage and support reflective practitioners to succeed in a situated learning environment.

3.6   Provide Feedback

As part of the reflective process and as motivation for reflection-in-action, feedback within the situation is essential. Jordan (2010) found that novice nurses who received feedback during the experience gained an awareness of alternative methods and diverse perspectives that widened personal perspectives, exposing areas of weakness. This feedback helps practitioners bring new perspectives to future novel experiences and, through reflection-in-action, better adjust to situations. Seibert (1999) found feedback is essential and occurs as a result of one's performance outcomes, from personal reflection, and from critique provided by experts and peers within the experience. Furthermore, he found that incorporating feedback within situated learning will provide learners with immediate information that enhances the ability to reflect-in-action and understand the results of engaging in the experience as a reflective practitioner.

References

Austin, Z., Gregory, P. A. M., & Chiu, S. (2008). Use of reflection-in-action and self-assessment to promote critical thinking among pharmacy students. *American Journal of Pharmaceutical Education, 72*(3), 48. https://doi.org/10.5688/aj720348.

Carroll, M. (2009). From mindless to mindful practice: On learning reflection in supervision. *Psychotherapy in Australia, 15*(4), 38.

Edwards, P. M. (2010). Theories-in-use and reflection-in-action: Core principles for LIS education. *Journal of Education for Library and Information Science, 51*(1), 18–29.

Eyler, J., & Giles, D. (1999). *Where's the learning in service-learning?* San Francisco: Jossey-Bass.

Goh, E. (2012). Integrating mindfulness and reflection in the teaching and learning of listening skills for undergraduate social work students in Singapore. *Social Work Education, 31*(5), 587–518. https://doi.org/10.1080/02615479.2011.579094.

Horton-Deutsch, S., Drew, B. L., & Beck-Coon, K. (2012). Mindful learners. In *Reflective practice transforming education and improving outcomes* (pp. 79–96). Indianapolis: Sigma Theta Tau International Honor Society of Nursing.

Jordan, S. (2010). Learning to be surprised: How to foster reflective practice in a high-reliability context. *Management Learning, 41*(4), 390–412. https://doi.org/10.1177/1350507609357388.

Jordan, S., Messner, M., & Becker, A. (2009). Reflection and mindfulness in organizations: Rationales and possibilities for integration. *Management Learning, 40*(4), 465–473. https://doi.org/10.1177/1350507609339687.

Keevers, L., & Treleaven, L. (2011). Organizing practices of reflection: A practice-based study. *Management Learning, 42*(5), 505–520. https://doi.org/10.1177/1350507610391592.

Mishna, F., & Bogo, M. (2007). Reflective practice in contemporary social work classrooms. *Journal of Social Work Education, 43*(3), 529–544.

Russell, A., Norton, C. L., Uriarte, J., & Wisner, B. (2011). Reflective teaching in social work education: Findings from a participatory action research study. *Social Work Education, 30*(4), 392–407. https://doi.org/10.1080/02615479.2010.500658.

Schön, D. A. (1983). *The reflective practitioner: How professionals think in action* (Vol. Book, Whole). New York: Basic Books.

Seibert, K. W. (1999). Reflection-in-action: Tools for cultivating on-the-job learning conditions. *Organizational Dynamics, 27*(3), 54–65. https://doi.org/10.1016/S0090-2616(99)90021-9.

Winn, W. (1993). Instructional design and situated learning: Paradox or partnership? *Educational Technology, 33*(3), 16.

Chapter 4
Mindfulness Strategies for Situated Learning

4.1 Mindfulness

One metacognitive strategy, mindfulness, not only has implications for enhancing reflection-in-action but also likely plays a principal role in high-road transfer as described by Salomon and Perkins (1989). Mindfulness is a method used to direct attention that has its roots in Eastern culture as a pillar of Buddhism meditation practices. Now widely practiced within Western culture, today a commonly accepted definition of mindfulness includes one's awareness and attention to the present moment and accepting the experience in a nonjudgmental way (Baer et al. 2004; Bush 2011; Davis 2014; Kabat-Zinn 1982). It is a heightened awareness of the present moment that allows one to be responsive rather than reactive because it quiets excess brain chatter. It can be thought of as the opposite of multitasking and is both a process and an outcome. One has to engage in mindful practice in order to develop a mindful awareness. Mindfulness, as compared to reflection, is a skill that allows one to control and direct his or her attention. Reflection, on the other hand, is "a generic term for those intellectual and affective activities in which individuals engage to explore their experiences in order to lead to new understandings and appreciations" (Boud et al. 1985). Therefore, reflection is a type of critical thinking, rather than a way of directing thoughts and attention as is the foundation of mindfulness.

Many associate mindfulness with religious connotations; however the very foundation of mindfulness rests in a pragmatic scientific way of thinking (Epstein 1999; Hart 2004). Everyone is mindful to some degree as it is an instinctive human capability (Kabat-Zinn 2003). Buddhist principles are associated with mindfulness as this culture originally taught and still emphasizes bringing mindfulness to daily life (Kabat-Zinn 2003). It is a skill that, when acquired, allows one to focus attention on the present moment and observe oneself including one's own personal behavior and inner dialogue (Goh 2012; Lynn 2010). The mind has a natural tendency to wander

© Association for Educational Communications and Technology 2018
A.M. Stoner, K.S. Cennamo, *Enhancing Reflection within Situated Learning*,
SpringerBriefs in Educational Communications and Technology,
https://doi.org/10.1007/978-3-319-70326-8_4

to other thoughts, memories, or feelings, often leaving behind much of what actually occurs in the present moment (Paulson et al. 2013; Kabat-Zinn 2003). Mindfulness creates a space to allow one to acknowledge the mind wandering but then actively redirect attention back to the present (Kabat-Zinn 1982).

From a cognitive perspective, the practice of mindfulness includes two major components: self-regulation of attention and an orientation to one's experience (Bishop et al. 2004). Self-regulation of attention involves both sustained attention to current experience and the flexibility to engage in switching attention back to the present after acknowledging the observed thought or feeling (Bishop et al. 2004). This allows one to directly experience the object or moment rather than experiencing it through the lens of personal emotions, beliefs, or expectations (Bishop et al. 2004). Creating space between preconceived prejudices to an experience and the present moment allows one to fully experience the moment and identify new and otherwise unnoticed details from a given event. In this respect, mindfulness is identified as a metacognitive skill both from a theoretical and neurological perspective (Bishop et al. 2004; Holas and Jankowski 2013). Intrinsic to mindful practice is a level of meta-awareness that allows individuals to deliberately monitor their own consciousness to percieve thoughts unrelated to a given task (Paulson et al. 2013; Holas and Jankowski 2013). Mindful individuals are aware that their mind is wandering and what their mind is observing and thinking. This inherently uses metacognitive skills that help manage cognitive processes including inhibitory control and cognitive flexibility (Holas and Jankowski 2013). Furthermore, both mindfulness and metacognition involve top-down processing that has been shown to be controlled by the prefrontal cortex in the brain (Paulson et al. 2013; Jankowski and Holas 2014). This neurological mechanism allows an individual to suppress one cognitive activity while activating another, a key feature of both mindfulness and metacognition (Jankowski and Holas 2014).

Orientation to one's experience refers more to the key piece of mindfulness: attitude (Bishop et al. 2004; Shapiro 2009). It is not only enough to direct one's attention, but how one directs attention is essential. With mindful awareness, as the mind wanders, an attitude of curiosity, openness, and acceptance is required (Bishop et al. 2004; Shapiro 2009; Kabat-Zinn 2003). Siegel (2007) describes this awareness as approaching a situation with curiosity, openness, acceptance, and love (COAL). Without these attitudinal qualities, it is likely that one will bring judgment, personal emotions, and preconceived expectations to a given experience. With a level of openness, compassion, and kindness, one is able to become fully open to whatever the present moment brings (Shapiro 2009). Possessing the proper attitude will help one avoid aspects of the experience, increase an ability for self-observation, and recognize cognitive and affective qualities of the experience (Bishop et al. 2004).

4.2   Mindfulness in Education

There has been a large interest in the application of mindfulness across disciplines, especially for clinical and psychological treatment. Mindfulness approaches such as mindfulness-based stress reduction and dialectical behavior therapy are often used to help patients with a variety of clinical diagnoses including pain management, anxiety, depression, addiction, and many other behavioral disorders (Bishop et al. 2004; Shapiro 2009; Kabat-Zinn 2003, 1982). Additionally, mindfulness is increasingly being incorporated into educational curriculums across disciplines as an instructional strategy (Bush 2011; Lynn 2010). Educators and administrators have taken an interest in determining how being more patient in the classroom affects cognitive functions and learning outcomes (Bush 2011). As a result, several organizations have been established including the Center for Contemplative Mind in Society, the Association for Mindfulness in Education, and Mindfulness in Education Network, which have increased awareness and encouraged bringing mindfulness practices into the classroom (Davis 2014).

Mindfulness plays a different role in an educational setting as compared to clinical practice. According to Stewart (2010), practicing mindfulness allows students to approach learning with cognitive flexibility, preventing mindless automated behavior and enhancing the ability to fully embrace the moment for future transfer of knowledge. Ritchhart and Perkins (2000) describe the role of mindfulness in education:

> Consequently, the real educational potential for mindfulness lies not in raising test scores but in addressing some of the other intractable problems of education such as the flexible transfer of skills and knowledge to new contexts, the development of deep understanding, student motivation and engagements, the ability to think critically and creatively, and the development of more self-directed learners.

Within the context of education, Langer (2000) defines mindfulness as "a flexible state of mind in which we are actively engaged in the present, noticing new things and sensitive to context" (p.220). When mindful, learners will draw new distinctions and notice novelty within a situation with behavior guided by rules and routines but not predetermined by them. This differs from what the author refers to a mindlessness way of learning where thoughts and behavior are governed merely by previously programmed knowledge that blinds the learner to only one possible perspective or solution. Throughout her extensive research, Langer has found many benefits of mindfulness within education and believes mindlessness is a result of the way content is delivered to the learners.

In two influential papers, Langer and her colleagues reported that incorporating a mindful way of delivering instruction increased learners' level of creativity when facing novel situations and spontaneously utilizing knowledge from a previous experience (Langer et al. 1989; Langer and Piper 1987). In each of these studies, the experimental group recieved "mindful" instruction where the information was delivered in a conditional manner using words such as "could be," "perhaps," or "from one perspective." The control group received information that was more absolute and less conditional.

In Langer and Piper's (1987) three experiments, the reseachers recruited an equal number of male and female Harvard undergraduate students. Participants were introduced to unfamiliar objects in either a "mindful", conditional manner, where the function or need for the object was flexible, or in a "mindless" or unconditional manner, where one absolute function for the object was provided. After instruction had taken place, the researchers introduced a scenario where there was a need for an object for assistance that the object currently present could not explicitly fulfill. In all three experiments, those students introduced to the unfamiliar object in a mindful conditional manner were able to provide a creative solution to the problem using the object in a novel way, whereas the control group was not. Individuals were evaluated based on behavioral responses, and groups were compared using Chi-square analyses.

Similarly, Langer et al. (1989) conducted a series of three experiments with various age groups. In each experiment, groups were again either given conditional, considered mindful, or unconditional, considered mindless, instruction. After the instruction, the participants had to carry out a task such as writing a type of poem, completing an exam, or delivering a training module. Results were evaluated using three raters to evaluate creativity, performance, and overall level of mindfulness. Those students taught from a mindful perspective were able to use the information in a creative manner to develop solutions, while those students taught from an absolute perspective were able to recite the information they had learned but were limited in applying the knowledge in a spontaneous or creative manner. While these studies included both college students and children, and the experiments reported in Langer and Piper (1987) focused only on college students, all of the studies found similar results.

Mindfulness in education has also been shown to increase attention, result in a greater level of personal liking and meaning for the content material, and improve memory (Langer 1997). In one experimental study of children (Carson et al. 2001) and one experimental study of adults (Levy et al. 2001), participants in the mindful group were asked to view objects (pictures and maps) from multiple perspectives, while the participants in the control groups were not given any direction on how to focus their attention. As a result, those who were able to mindfully attend to the objects demonstrated improved attention and also improved memory of the objects they observed. It was concluded those in the mindful groups were able to draw on information from multiple perspectives, increasing their memory, rather than have one fixed viewpoint of the object.

In addition to these early studies on mindfulness in education, more recently, benefits resulting from direct instruction in mindfulness practices have been described in the literature (Bush 2011). In an examination and synthesis of recent college courses, including several academic disciplines that all were introducing mindfulness within their classroom practices, the author found that, although each instructor approached the utilization of mindfulness in education somewhat differently depending on the intended outcome, across these courses, professors reported the following changes in the learners: increased concentration, greater ability for synthetic thinking, increased cognitive flexibility, and a greater appreciation for the learning process (Bush 2011). The results varied across each example and were self-reported in a focus group interview setting by instructors who were implementing mindfulness in their courses.

Similarly, in a sociology course, a research study incorporated formal mindfulness practices with the aim to help increase understanding of the complex relationship between society and the individual (Song and Muschert 2014). At the beginning of each class, the students were introduced to a different mindfulness practice and then actively participated in the practice of the day. Examples included stillness practices, visualization, creative practices such as journaling and contemplative art, deep listening, walking meditation, and creating a personal space. Students not only reported that mindfulness was a positive experience in relation to their learning, but they also developed an enhanced level of personal awareness and a broader perspective and understanding of the content.

Finally, in a study of social work students who were working in an experiential learning environment in the field, mindfulness training was incorporated to help students face the stressors and increase cognitive support during their experiences (Birnbaum 2008). Using qualitative analyses, the researchers found that students who were using mindfulness training during their experiences reported an increased self-awareness, increased emotional support for stressors in their field experiences, and a greater personal insight into their professional self-concept than prior to having participated in regular mindfulness practices throughout the course (Birnbaum 2008).

4.3   Mindfulness as an Instructional Strategy

While sometimes confused as merely a form of relaxation, mindfulness is a cognitive skill that can be developed and acquired with the appropriate training and practice (Bishop et al. 2004). There are many methods to help learners develop mindfulness skills that could be helpful in implementing mindful learning as an instructional strategy for situated learning. Mindful learning requires a very active role of the learner and therefore requires certain features of the learner summarized by Siegel (2007) to include "openness to novelty, alertness to distinction, sensitivity to different contexts, implicit, if not explicit awareness of multiple perspectives, and orientation to the present" (p.237).

Shapiro (2009) developed a model of mindfulness training that encompasses these elements through three main themes: *attention, attitude, and intention*. From a cognitive perspective, mindfulness is an *attention* regulation skill; therefore one element of the model includes attention to both internal and external experiences within the present moment (Shapiro 2009). Epstein (2003a) expands on the importance of attention in his conceptual model of mindfulness for the training of medical students and practicing physicians. Learners must be able to engage in critical observation of themselves and become aware of their own perceptions and biases during a given situation. In keeping an openness to novelty and alertness to distinction (Siegel 2007), this includes looking for both the familiar and unexpected within an experience and solving a problem (Epstein 2003a).

The next key feature of mindful practice is *attitude* (Shapiro 2009). As supported in the extensive research of Langer described above, for mindful learning to occur, learners need to embrace critical curiosity and an openness for new information and awareness of multiple perspectives (Siegel 2007; Langer 1997). Critical curiosity involves inviting doubt and a flexibility to pursue situations from multiple perspectives (Epstein 2003a). When the learners view the situation free of premature cognitive commitments, they have a greater ability to examine information from new perspectives in order to create new schemas or categories for which the novel experiences will align (Langer 1997). This, according to Epstein (2003a), is maintaining a "beginners mind" and includes tolerating doubt and uncertainty in order to maintain openness.

Finally, the *intention* of the learner in engaging in mindfulness is important (Shapiro 2009). A learner's sensitivity to context, openness in a nonjudgmental way to the present, and staying within the present in order to engage in mindfulness will result in more mindful learning (Epstein 2003a; Langer 1997; Siegel 2007). A learner must have intention to engage in mindful practice as it will not occur naturally.

While the existing literature on mindfulness within education is limited, there have been recommendations and applications of methods that could be utilized to develop mindfulness within an instructional setting. As recommended for training mindfulness skills in other disciplines, in order to achieve mindful learning, a foundation of mindfulness skills should be developed and then carried forward for application into everyday activities (Kabat-Zinn 1982).

Mindfulness can be incorporated into instruction using both formal and informal mindfulness practices (Carmody and Baer 2008; Pezzolesi et al. 2013; Shapiro 2009). It is often the case that formal mindfulness meditation practices will be used to help learners build the foundation for mindfulness skills in order to apply mindfulness in everyday activities through informal mindfulness practices (Carmody and Baer 2008; Pezzolesi et al. 2013; Shapiro 2009). Without formal practice, it is difficult to achieve the ability to engage in informal practice. Formal practices include activities such as sitting meditation, body scan, yoga, or breathing exercises. Informal practices, which are more consistent with what would be utilized in situated learning, include applying mindfulness skills to any routine activity in which one is engaging and attempting to become aware of all sensations one is experiencing. This can include eating, walking, doing chores, or engaging with others (Carmody and Baer 2008; Pezzolesi et al. 2013; Shapiro 2009).

Based on techniques to build mindfulness skills within a clinical setting, within an instructional environment, formal mindfulness practice can begin with simple formal practices such as attention to breath until attention has become stable and, as the learners build their skills, allow their attention to expand to other objects to include all physical and mental events within the room (Kabat-Zinn 1982). When individual mindfulness skills have been developed, group mindfulness practices can also be used. Epstein (2003b) developed a method of effectively teaching mindfulness that includes priming, availability, asking reflective questions, active engagement, modeling, practice, praxis, and assessment, intended to improve health professionals' practices. Additional methods that have been utilized for incorporating mindfulness in learning environments include building an environment of self-observation, reflective journaling and discussion for inviting curiosity, modeling while thinking out loud, experiential learning, and intuitive writings (Epstein 2003b; Birnbaum 2008). From a content delivery perspective, mindful learning requires conditional instruction, in contrast to an absolute perspective, in order to create an openness to other perspectives and a sensitivity to the context of information (Langer 1993, 1997, 2000).

As described above, mindfulness as an instructional strategy can provide situated learners with the ability to focus their attention on the present moment and maintain an openness to different perspectives, helping them adapt to the ill-structured nature of situated learning. This is an essential metacognitive skill that instructional designers could integrate to provide support for learners in an unpredictable situated learning environment and to enhance learners' ability to act as reflective practitioners within the community of practice. As described by Horton-Deutsch et al. (2012), when mindful, "learners bring clarity to what they are sensing, feeling, thinking, wanting, and willing to do. Integrating mindfulness into educational pursuits lays the foundation for reflective learning" (p.81).

4.4 Mindfulness and Reflection-in-Action

Mindfulness and reflection-in-action are intimately connected, and when integrated, it has been previously suggested that mindfulness is one strategy that could be used to improve reflection-in-action (Jordan et al. 2009; Pezzolesi et al. 2013). In a study that applied auto-ethnography and action research methods, the authors examined how medical professionals utilize mindfulness in both their professional and personal lives (Nugent et al. 2011). Based on their findings, the researchers concluded mindfulness is facilitative of reflective practice. Qualitative analyses revealed the participants reported that mindfulness enhanced reflection by offering a place to stop and think, deepened their relationship with themselves, and provided clarity for them to perceive things in a different way, changing the way they responded and behaved within a situation.

It has also been suggested that mindfulness enhances reflection-in-action by playing an influential role in an individual's decision making (Epstein 1999). In an extensive synthesis of literature within social work education, Mishna and Bogo (2007) investigated how mindfulness and reflection-in-action can benefit social work instructors as they teach socially sensitive content to diverse classrooms. In the development of their framework, the authors concluded the integration of these principles enhances the instructor's ability to adjust to conflict within the classroom through improved reactive decisions when facing conflict. When engaging in mindful reflection-in-action, they have the ability to respond with creative and novel solutions rather than in an automated habitual way that may impede the trusting culture of the classroom. Similarly, however not formally tested, based on evidence within medical education practice, it has been suggested that mindful reflective practice could allow healthcare professionals to relieve stress, increase their attention and awareness, and consequently, improve treatment for patients by reducing medications errors that resulted from poor attention and automated behavior (Pezzolesi et al. 2013).

Additionally, mindfulness integrated with reflective practice enhances overall learning and performance outcomes, as it provides learners with the ability to gain a better understanding as a result of experience in the present moment (Horton-Deutsch et al. 2012). In a series of two studies which integrated mindfulness and reflection within a social work classroom curriculum, researchers examined how mindfulness and reflection affect the learners' ability to develop and apply active learning skills when working with a patient, a foundational strategy for social work practice (Goh 2012). After qualitative analyses of both group and personal reflections, the results indicated that when mindfulness and reflection were combined within an instructional environment, learners reported an enhanced awareness of poor habits that hindered their active listening skills and the ability to adjust their attention to improve performance within the present moment. In addition, learners reported an enhanced personal awareness and stronger learning outcomes as a result of engaging in mindfulness and reflective practices.

While not empirically tested, other benefits of incorporating mindfulness for reflection-in-action have been identified and described within the literature. Horton-Deutsch et al. (2012) indicate that mindfulness practice enhances reflection-in-action as it can free the learner from previously engrained perceptions and schema, tacit knowledge, and automated habitual behavior (Horton-Deutsch et al. 2012). This creates an openness which allows for learners to reflect-in-action in analyzing the experience as it occurs in order to develop creative solutions that will allow them to adapt to novel situations and solve complex problems. When mindful, learners and practitioners have a personal awareness that allows them to access information that would normally be outside of their perspective, allowing for deeper reflective thinking in reflection-in-action (Horton-Deutsch et al. 2012; Bishop et al. 2004). When learners engage in reflection-in-action supported by mindfulness, they are able to find more meaning in the present moment which in turn enhances the meaning-making process when they engage in reflection-on-action (Horton-Deutsch et al. 2012). As situated learners act as practitioners within a community of practice, it is essential for learners to have skills that allow them to succeed as practitioners by facing ill-structured problems and novel situations. Based on the benefits of the integration of these two concepts as indicted in the existing literature, mindfulness and reflection-in-action are two instructional strategies that, if incorporated into the design of the learning experience, could enhance a situated learning environment.

As described above, mindfulness strategies have been integrated across many disciplines including education. Several mindfulness strategies are apparent in the

Table 4.1 Strategies for mindfulness in education

Strategies	Methods to support incorporating the strategy
1. Provide an orientation to mindfulness (Birnbaum 2008; Bohecker et al. 2014; Crumley and Schutz 2011; Epstein 2003b; Trunnell 1996; Shapiro 2009; Carroll 2009)	• Include an introduction to what constitutes mindfulness and methods on how to become mindful learners (Birnbaum 2008; Bohecker et al. 2014; Crumley and Schutz 2011; Epstein 2003b; Trunnell 1996)
2. Include formal and informal mindfulness practices (Diaz 2011; Crumley and Schutz 2011; Mapel 2012; Trunnell 1996)	• Build a foundation for informal practices through formal practices (Diaz 2011; Crumley and Schutz 2011; Mapel 2012; Trunnell 1996) • Integrate informal into everyday experience (Birnbaum 2008)
3. Deliver instruction in a mindful or conditional way (Anglin et al. 2008; Langer et al. 1989; Langer and Piper 1987; Ryu and Lee 2015; Sherretz 2011)	• Present material from multiple perspectives (Anglin et al. 2008; Langer et al. 1989; Langer and Piper 1987; Ryu and Lee 2015; Sherretz 2011) • Use conditional language to maintain cognitive flexibility (Anglin et al. 2008; Langer et al. 1989; Langer and Piper 1987; Ryu and Lee 2015; Sherretz 2011)

literature that transfer to situated learning environments to help promote reflection. As illustrated in Table 4.1 and discussed below, the following strategies can be incorporated when designing for reflection within situated learning, particularly to promote reflection-in-action: providing an orientation to mindfulness, including both formal and informal mindfulness practices, and delivering instruction in a mindful or conditional way.

4.5 Providing an Orientation to Mindfulness

While we are all mindful to some degree, most learners do not have the skills or training to naturally engage in mindfulness. Therefore, research has indicated in order for learners to engage in mindfulness during a situated learning experience, they must first be oriented to what constitutes mindfulness and strategies to learn how to become mindful learners (Birnbaum 2008; Crumley and Schutz 2011; Epstein 2003b; Trunnell 1996). A literature review on mindfulness used in counseling training education presents evidence that indicates that this will set the stage for mindfulness, helping learners develop a mindful awareness and learn how to apply mindfulness within practice (Bohecker et al. 2014). Providing an orientation to mindfulness builds the attention, attitude, and intention required for mindfulness practice (Shapiro 2009). Additionally, it prepares students to be present in the moment, clearing space and building cognitive flexibility in order to engage in reflection during the experience (Carroll 2009; Bohecker et al. 2014).

4.6   Informal Mindfulness and Formal Mindfulness

Mindfulness can be incorporated into instruction through either formal or informal practices. Within education, formal mindfulness practices most often include guided meditation through body scan (learning to direct attention by focusing on the body in the present moment from head to toe) or through sitting meditation (focusing on breath and learning to focus on feelings, sensations, and the surroundings). Informal practices, which are more consistent with what would be utilized in situated learning, include applying mindfulness skills to any routine activity in which one is engaging and attempting to become aware of all sensations one is experiencing. This can include eating, walking, doing chores, or engaging with others.

Included as part of the orientation to mindfulness should be both formal and informal mindfulness practices. Most often, formal mindfulness meditation practices will be used to help learners build the foundation for mindfulness skills in order to apply mindfulness in everyday activities through informal mindfulness practices. An experimental study that assessed the effects of brief formal mindfulness practices through body scan on perceived attention found that music students reported experiencing decreased distraction and increased attention during learning and performance, as compared to the control group (Diaz 2011). Other educational research studies that assessed the effects of guided sitting meditation found learners reported attribution outcomes that indicated learners (1) were more present during the experiential learning process, decreasing boredom (Trunnell 1996), (2) had an increased focus and better understanding of the course content (Crumley and Schutz 2011), and (3) acquired a skill to help manage stressful situations which enhanced learning according to quantitative and qualitative responses from the students (Mapel 2012).

Without formal practice, it is difficult to achieve the ability to engage in informal mindfulness practice (Carmody and Baer 2008; Pezzolesi et al. 2013; Shapiro 2009). Research on informal mindfulness practices incorporated into experiential learning has found that students who were engaged in mindfulness training during their experiences reported an increased self-awareness, increased emotional support for stressors in their field experiences, and a greater personal insight into their professional self-concept than prior to having participated in regular mindfulness practices throughout the course (Birnbaum 2008).

4.7   Mindful Instruction

In order for learners to reflect-in-action, they need to have a level of cognitive flexibility that allows them to adapt to surprises and unfamiliar experiences. Mindful instruction, or presenting material in a conditional manner, helps students increase cognitive flexibility by allowing students to see content and experiences from multiple perspectives or presentations (Anglin et al. 2008; Langer et al. 1989; Langer and Piper 1987; Ryu and Lee 2015; Sherretz 2011). Similar to an orientation to mindfulness, mindful instruction builds the foundation for mindful learners who are able to reflect in the present moment by preparing them cognitively for future situated learning experiences. Several experimental studies have illustrated that when instruction is delivered in a mindful versus a mindless manner, learners have increased cognitive flexibility (Langer and Piper 1987; Ryu and Lee 2015), the ability to adapt and use creative solutions to novel situations (Langer et al. 1989; Langer and Piper 1987), and a more balanced attitude toward content and experiences (Anglin et al. 2008). These are all essential skills in creating learners with the ability to critically reflect in a situated learning experience.

References

Anglin, L. P., Pirson, M., & Langer, E. (2008). Mindful learning: A moderator of gender differences in mathematics performance. *Journal of Adult Development, 15*(3), 132–139. https://doi.org/10.1007/s10804-008-9043-x.

Baer, R. A., Smith, G. T., & Allen, K. B. (2004). Assessment of mindfulness by self-report: The Kentucky inventory of mindfulness skills. *Assessment, 11*(3), 191–206. https://doi.org/10.1177/1073191104268029.

Birnbaum, L. (2008). The use of mindfulness training to create an 'accompanying place' for social work students. *Social Work Education, 27*(8), 837–852. https://doi.org/10.1080/02615470701538330.

Bishop, S. R., Lau, M., Shapiro, S., Carlson, L., Anderson, N. D., Carmody, J., et al. (2004). Mindfulness: A proposed operational definition. *Clinical Psychology: Science and Practice, 11*(3), 230–241. https://doi.org/10.1093/clipsy.bph077.

Bohecker, L., Wathen, C., Wells, P., Salazar, B. M., & Vereen, L. G. (2014). Mindfully educating our future: The MESG curriculum for training emergent counselors. *The Journal for Specialists in Group Work, 39*(3), 257–273. https://doi.org/10.1080/01933922.2014.919046.

Boud, D., Keogh, R., & Walker, D. (1985). *Reflection, turning experience into learning* (Vol. Book, Whole). New York/London: Kogan Page.

Bush, M. (2011). Mindfulness in higher education. *Contemporary Buddhism, 12*(1), 183–197. https://doi.org/10.1080/14639947.2011.564838.

Carmody, J., & Baer, R. A. (2008). Relationships between mindfulness practice and levels of mindfulness, medical and psychological symptoms and well-being in a mindfulness-based stress reduction program. *Journal of Behavioral Medicine, 31*(1), 23–33. https://doi.org/10.1007/s10865-007-9130-7.

Carroll, M. (2009). From mindless to mindful practice: On learning reflection in supervision. *Psychotherapy in Australia, 15*(4), 38.

Carson, S., Shih, M., & Langer, E. (2001). Sit still and pay attention? *Journal of Adult Development, 8*(3), 183–188. https://doi.org/10.1023/A:1009594324594.

Crumley, G., & Schutz, H. (2011). *Short-duration mindfulness training with adult learners* (Vol. 22, pp. 37–42). Bowie: American Association for Adult and Continuing Education.

Davis, D. J. (2014). *Mindfulness in teaching, learning, and leadership: Implications for higher education.* Paper presented at the Clute Institute International Academic Conference, Orlando.

Diaz, F. M. (2011). Mindfulness, attention, and flow during music listening: An empirical investigation. *Psychology of Music, 41*(1), 42–58. https://doi.org/10.1177/0305735611415144.

Epstein, R. M. (1999). Mindful practice. *JAMA, 282*(9), 833–839. https://doi.org/10.1001/jama.282.9.833.

Epstein, R. M. (2003a). Mindful practice in action (I): Technical competence, evidence-based medicine, and relationship-centered care. *Families, Systems & Health, 21*(1), 1–9. https://doi.org/10.1037/h0089494.

Epstein, R. M. (2003b). Mindful practice in action (II): Cultivating habits of mind. *Families, Systems & Health, 21*(1), 11–17. https://doi.org/10.1037/h0089495.

Goh, E. (2012). Integrating mindfulness and reflection in the teaching and learning of listening skills for undergraduate social work students in Singapore. *Social Work Education, 31*(5), 587–518. https://doi.org/10.1080/02615479.2011.579094.

Hart, T. (2004). Opening the contemplative mind in the classroom. *Journal of Transformative Education, 2*(1), 28–46.

Holas, P., & Jankowski, T. (2013). A cognitive perspective on mindfulness. *International Journal of Psychology, 48*(3), 232–243. https://doi.org/10.1080/00207594.2012.658056.

Horton-Deutsch, S., Drew, B. L., & Beck-Coon, K. (2012). Mindful learners. In *Reflective practice transforming education and improving outcomes* (pp. 79–96). Indianapolis: Sigma Theta Tau International Honor Society of Nursing.

Jankowski, T., & Holas, P. (2014). Metacognitive model of mindfulness. *Consciousness and Cognition, 28*, 64–80. https://doi.org/10.1016/j.concog.2014.06.005.

Jordan, S., Messner, M., & Becker, A. (2009). Reflection and mindfulness in organizations: Rationales and possibilities for integration. *Management Learning, 40*(4), 465–473. https://doi.org/10.1177/1350507609339687.

Kabat-Zinn, J. (1982). An outpatient program in behavioral medicine for chronic pain patients based on the practice of mindfulness meditation: Theoretical considerations and preliminary results. *General Hospital Psychiatry, 4*(1), 33–47. https://doi.org/10.1016/0163-8343(82)90026-3.

Kabat-Zinn, J. (2003). Mindfulness-based interventions in context: Past, present, and future. *Clinical Psychology Science and Practice, 10*(2), 144–156. https://doi.org/10.1093/clipsy/bpg016.

Langer, E. J. (1993). A mindful education. *Educational Psychologist, 28*(1), 43–50. https://doi.org/10.1207/s15326985ep2801_4.

Langer, E. J. (1997). *The power of mindful learning* (Vol. Book, Whole). Reading: Addison-Wesley.

Langer, E. J. (2000). Mindful learning. *Current Directions in Psychological Science, 9*(6), 220–223. https://doi.org/10.1111/1467-8721.00099.

Langer, E. J., & Piper, A. I. (1987). The prevention of mindlessness. *Journal of Personality and Social Psychology, 53*(2), 280–287. https://doi.org/10.1037//0022-3514.53.2.280.

Langer, E. J., Hatem, M., Joss, J., & Howell, M. (1989). Conditional teaching and mindful learning. *Creativity Research Journal, 2*(3), 139–150. https://doi.org/10.1080/10400418909534311.

Levy, B. R., Jennings, P., & Langer, E. J. (2001). Improving attention in old age. *Journal of Adult Development, 8*(3), 189–192. https://doi.org/10.1023/A:1009546408665.

Lynn, R. (2010). Mindfulness in social work education. *Social Work Education, 29*(3), 289–304. https://doi.org/10.1080/02615470902930351.

Mapel, T. (2012). Mindfulness and education: Students' experience of learning mindfulness in a tertiary classroom. *New Zealand Journal of Educational Studies, 47*(1), 19.

Mishna, F., & Bogo, M. (2007). Reflective practice in contemporary social work classrooms. *Journal of Social Work Education, 43*(3), 529–544.

Nugent, P., Moss, D., Barnes, R., & Wilks, J. (2011). Clear (ing) space: Mindfulness-based reflective practice. *Reflective Practice, 12*(1), 1–13.

Paulson, S., Davidson, R., Jha, A., & Kabat-Zinn, J. (2013). Becoming conscious: The science of mindfulness. *Annals of the New York Academy of Sciences, 1303*(1), 87–104. https://doi.org/10.1111/nyas.12203.

Pezzolesi, C., Ghaleb, M., Kostrzewski, A., & Dhillon, S. (2013). Is mindful reflective practice the way forward to reduce medication errors? *International Journal of Pharmacy Practice, 21*(6), 413–416. https://doi.org/10.1111/ijpp.12031.

Ritchhart, R., & Perkins, D. N. (2000). Life in the mindful classroom: Nurturing the disposition of mindfulness. *Journal of Social Issues, 56*(1), 27–47.

Ryu, J., & Lee, D.-m. (2015). Mindful learning in geography: Cultivating balanced attitudes toward regions. *Journal of Geography, 114*(5), 197–210. https://doi.org/10.1080/00221341.2 015.1046897.

Salomon, G., & Perkins, D. N. (1989). Rocky roads to transfer: Rethinking mechanism of a neglected phenomenon. *Educational Psychologist, 24*(2), 113–142.

Shapiro, S. L. (2009). *The art and science of mindfulness: Integrating mindfulness into psychology and the helping professions* (Vol. Book, Whole). Washington D.C.: American Psychological Association.

Sherretz, C. E. (2011). Mindfulness in education: Case studies of mindful teachers and their teaching practices. *Journal of Thought, 46*(3–4), 79–96.

Siegel, D. J. (2007). *The mindful brain: Reflection and attunement in the cultivation of well-being* (Vol. Book, Whole). New York: W.W. Norton.

Song, K. Y., & Muschert, G. W. (2014). Opening the contemplative mind in the sociology classroom. *Humanity and Society, 38*(3), 314–338. https://doi.org/10.1177/0160597614537794.

Stewart, T. (2010). Opening up service-learning reflection by turning inward: Developing mindful learneres through contemplation. In *Problematizing service-learning critical reflections for development and action* (pp. 37–70). Charlotte: Information Age Publishing.

Trunnell, E. P. (1996). Optimizing an outdoor experience for experiential learning by decreasing boredom through mindfulness training. *The Journal of Experimental Education, 19*(1), 43.

Chapter 5
A Conceptual Model Incorporating Mindfulness to Enhance Reflection in a Situated Learning Environment

5.1 A Conceptual Model

The following is a conceptual model incorporating mindfulness to promote reflection-in-action within a situated learning environment. Conceptual models are analytic in nature and aim to identify, define, and describe the relationships among variables (Richey 1986, 2005). The purpose of this conceptual model is to bring together conclusions from current empirical literature from three fields to illustrate how to enhance reflection in situated learning through reflection-in-action and mindfulness. By integrating strategies to enhance reflective practice for situated learners, instructional designers will be able to address some of the challenges faced when designing for the variable and uncertain environments that arise within situated learning.

This model includes key elements for promoting reflection before, during, and after the situated learning experience, along with complimentary mindfulness strategies throughout the model, as supported within the literature. As illustrated in Fig. 5.1, it is organized based on three phases of reflection: reflection-before-action (R-B-A), reflection-in-action (R-I-A), and reflection-on-action (R-O-A). Mindfulness strategies to promote R-I-A, along with key characteristics to facilitate reflection in situated learning, are included for each phase of the model. Examples of ways to incorporate each strategy are provided to aid in the application and usability of the model. Resources are provided in Appendix A for further information on learning and incorporating formal mindfulness within an educational environment. Additionally, associated outcomes are provided in Table 5.1 to illustrate the benefits of creating an environment that promotes R-I-A during situated learning and to provide evidence for including mindfulness as an instructional strategy for metacognitive support to enhance R-I-A.

© Association for Educational Communications and Technology 2018
A.M. Stoner, K.S. Cennamo, *Enhancing Reflection within Situated Learning*,
SpringerBriefs in Educational Communications and Technology,
https://doi.org/10.1007/978-3-319-70326-8_5

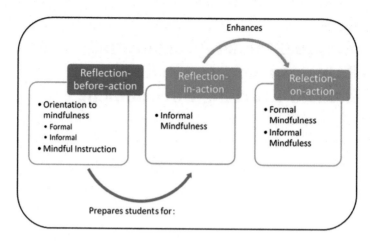

Fig. 5.1 A conceptual model incorporating mindfulness to enhance reflection in a situated learning environment

Table 5.1 A conceptual model incorporating mindfulness to enhance reflection in a situated learning environment including associated outcomes

Strategies	Outcomes
Phase 1 – reflection-before-action	
Create a reflective environment	• Encourages reflection early and often for the learners (Carroll 2009; Granville and Dison 2005) • Brings out students' awareness of personal assumptions and beliefs that may impede cognitive flexibility (Eyler 2001; Stewart 2010) • Prepares students to be observant and thoughtful and to address surprises (Eyler 2001; Carroll 2009) • Creates a culture that allows a student to learn to reflect spontaneously (Boudreau et al. 2014; Herrington et al. 2014)
Utilize mindful instruction	• Increases cognitive flexibility (Langer and Piper 1987; Ryu and Lee 2015) • Increases creativity within a learning situation (Langer et al. 1989; Langer and Piper 1987) • Creates more balanced attitudes toward content and situations (Anglin et al. 2008)

Provide an orientation to mindfulness
    Formal mindfulness
    Informal mindfulness
	• Clears cognitive space for reflection (Carroll 2009)
	• Provides a foundation for learners to engage in informal mindfulness practices (Carmody and Baer 2008)
	• Prepares students to become present within an experience
	• Builds the attention, attitude, and intention required for mindfulness practice (Shapiro 2009)

(continued)

Table 5.1   (continued)

Strategies	Outcomes
Phase 2 – Reflection-in-action	
Create a learning environment to enhance reflection-in-action	• Enhances the quality and level of reflection (Croker et al. 1998; Granville and Dison 2005; Huisman and Edwards 2011; Ovens and Tinning 2009; Stalmeijer et al. 2009) • Provides an authentic situation in which students can relate (Croker et al. 1998; Granville and Dison 2005) • Helps learners reflect spontaneously and independently (Boudreau et al. 2014; Herrington et al. 2014)
Create an environment that allows for social interaction with others to promote reflection-in-action	• Allows for personal comparison and immediate reflection (Croker et al. 1998; Eick et al. 2003; Russell et al. 2011) • Facilitates reflection-in-action through personal comparison and adjustment in practice (Bell and Mladenovic 2015; Edwards 2010) • Promotes interactive and innovative reflective practitioners (Jordan 2010; Seibert 1999)
Engage in informal mindfulness to promote reflection-in-action	• Helps manage stressful and unfamiliar situations in a more productive manner (Birnbaum 2008; Bohecker et al. 2014; Mapel 2012) • Increases attention and focus with less distraction for the learner (Bush 2011; Crumley and Schutz 2011; Diaz 2011) • Enhances interest, engagement, and involvement from the learner (Trunnell 1996) • Enhances self-awareness (Birnbaum 2008; Song and Muschert 2014) • Allows for a sustained cognitive flexibility (Bush 2011) • Helps meet demands of situation (Ovens and Tinning 2009) • Meets demands of situation by limiting distractions or other tensions (Mishna and Bogo 2007) • Allows one to detect thoughts and behaviors in order to better engage in and respond to a situation (Goh 2012; Keevers and Treleaven 2011) • Enhances ability to become reflective practitioners (Russell et al. 2011; Keevers and Treleaven 2011)

Provide feedback
   Instructor identifies strengths and weaknesses
   Students ask questions throughout the experience
   Provide results of performance from peers and instructor
	• Helps students see the value in reflection (Stalmeijer et al. 2009)
	• Gives students support when struggling with difficult situations (Herrington et al. 2014)
	• Identifies alternative procedures and perspectives exposing areas in need of improvement (Jordan 2010)
	• Provides immediate information that helps one reflect-in-action (Seibert 1999)

Phase 3 – Reflection-on-action	
Provide the opportunity for learners to reflect on the practice	• Students reevaluate the situation and begin to integrate new knowledge for future application (Herrington and Oliver 2000) • Helps process new information gained from the experience (Seibert 1999)
Learners engage in formal mindfulness	• Learners attend to the reflective process to reevaluate and improve future performance (Horton-Deutsch et al. 2012)

5.2   Reflection-Before-Action

While R-I-A and R-O-A are important within a situated learning environment, engaging in R-B-A is also important (Fig. 5.2). Evidence suggests that prior to engaging in the learning experience, reflection can help students learn to be observant, thoughtful, and develop strategies to address surprises or conflict they may encounter (Eyler 2001; Stewart 2010). These are essential skills in being able to reflect-in-action within practice. In order to facilitate R-B-A, several strategies can be incorporated into the instructional design. These strategies are described below along with examples of how to apply to these strategies (see Table 5.2).

5.2.1   Create a Reflective Environment

The first strategy addresses the learning context and environment. Learners are not always naturally reflective and often need guidance to initially promote reflection. Therefore, prior to engaging in situated learning, it is important to build a reflective environment: an environment that incorporates and encourages reflection throughout the learning experience. Creating a reflective environment will help learners incorporate many strategies that result in outcomes important for situated learning. Research has found, when learners are encouraged to engage in reflection and feel comfortable within the learning environment, the instructor can aid them in engaging in reflection earlier and more frequently throughout the learning process (Granville and Dison 2005; Carroll 2009). While students often need guidance to become effective reflective practitioners, the ultimate goal is for them to reflect spontaneously. According to Boudreau et al. (2014) and Herrington et al. (2014), creating this type of environment will help reflection become part of a student's normal routine within the learning experience. As a result, the student will be more likely to engage in spontaneous reflection. Additionally, as is important in engaging in mindfulness, learners are able to reflect-in-action when they maintain a level of cognitive flexibility, a cognitive ability that "involves the selective use of knowledge to adaptively fit the needs of understanding and decision making in a particular situation" (Spiro, Coulson, and Daniel 1988, p.5). Creating a reflective environment in which the learners feel comfortable engaging in discussion allows them to become aware of personal assumptions and beliefs that may impede their ability to remain open, aware, and creative within the learning situation (Eyler 2001). In order to create a reflective environment, instructors could provide regular encouragement to engage in reflection, ensure they are providing guidance for reflection, create an open and safe environment for student reflection, and aid students in becoming aware of personal assumptions and beliefs (Table 5.2).

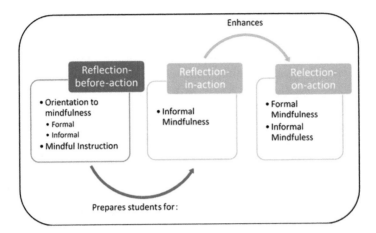

Fig. 5.2 A conceptual model of reflection in situated learning highlighting reflection-before-action

Table 5.2 Examples to incorporate strategies within phase 1: reflection-before-action

Create a reflective environment	• Encourage learners to engage in reflection • Provide guidance for reflection • Create an open and safe environment for student reflection • Help students become aware of personal assumptions and beliefs
Utilize mindful instruction	• Deliver instruction in a conditional manner • Utilize conditional language • Present material from multiple perspectives • Develop sensitivity by giving learners opportunity for exploration • Provide learners opportunities to explore additional possibilities • Introduce ambiguity that requires additional processing by the leaner

Provide an orientation to mindfulness	• Introduce what constitutes mindfulness and methods on how to become mindful learners
	• Begin with formal mindfulness exercises:
	  – Body scan
	  – Sitting meditation
	  – Yoga
	  – Breathing exercises
	• Expand to informal mindfulness exercises:
	  – Engage in mindfulness during any routine activity

5.2.2   Utilize Mindful Instruction

Another strategy to incorporate during R-B-A is delivering instruction in a mindful versus a mindless manner. Mindful instruction involves presenting content in a conditional manner that allows learners to see a topic or situation from many different perspectives rather than only understanding it from one perspective or for one purpose. In addition to using conditional language and presenting material from multiple perspectives, Ritchhart and Perkins (2000) have suggested three additional instructional methods for cultivating mindful learners: develop sensitivity by giving learners opportunity for exploration with an expectation of finding results of value, exploring additional possibilities, and introducing ambiguity that require additional processing by the learner. These strategies prevent a mindlessness way of learning where our thoughts and behavior are governed merely by previously programmed knowledge, blinding the learner to only one possible perspective or solution (Langer 2000). Research has suggested that using mindful instruction will help learners in the reflection-in-action process as it increases cognitive flexibility (Langer and Piper 1987; Ryu and Lee 2015), increases creativity within a learning situation (Langer et al. 1989; Langer and Piper 1987), and creates more balanced attitudes toward content and situations (Anglin et al. 2008).

5.2.3   Orientation to Mindfulness

In order for learners to become mindful during the situated learning experience, they must have an orientation to mindfulness that can be incorporated by engaging in R-B-A within the instructional setting. As with reflection, it is likely that learners will not have the ability to naturally engage in mindfulness practices. Therefore, providing an introduction to what constitutes mindfulness and how it can benefit learners will be an important first step in building the foundation for mindful practice. Incorporating opportunities for learners to actually engage in mindful practice, as they will within the situated learning environment, will enhance their ability to practice mindfulness regularly. First introducing and practicing formal mindfulness and then expanding to engage in informal mindfulness will help students develop the basic skills that they will carry forward into the situated learning experience. Formal practices include activities such as sitting meditation, body scan, yoga, or breathing exercises. Informal practices, which are more consistent with what would be utilized in situated learning, include applying mindfulness skills to any routine activity in which one is engaging and attempting to become aware of all sensations one is experiencing. This can include eating, walking, doing chores, or engaging with others (Carmody and Baer 2008; Pezzolesi et al. 2013; Shapiro 2009).

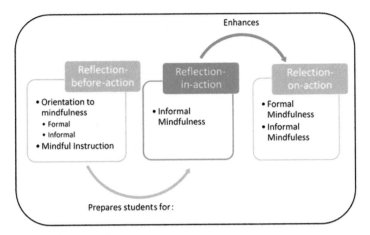

Fig. 5.3 A conceptual model of reflection in situated learning highlighting reflection-in-action

5.3   Reflection-in-Action

Once learners have had an orientation to mindfulness and have been immersed in a reflective environment which incorporates aspects of mindful instruction, they have the foundation to help them succeed as reflective practitioners when engaging in the situated learning experience (Fig. 5.3). Several key design features regarding the context and environment are important to include for R-I-A in situated learning as illustrated within the empirical evidence (Ovens and Tinning 2009; Granville and Dison 2005). These elements include creating an authentic learning environment (Boudreau et al. 2014; Herrington et al. 2014; Herrington and Oliver 2000; Croker et al. 1998), creating an experience that is longer in duration (Boudreau et al. 2014; Croker et al. 1998; Granville and Dison 2005; Huisman and Edwards 2011; Stalmeijer et al. 2009), and allowing for ample social interaction between the learner and his or her peers along with experts in the field (Bell and Mladenovic 2015; Croker et al. 1998; Edwards 2010; Eick et al. 2003; Herrington and Oliver 2000; Jordan 2010; Russell et al. 2011; Seibert 1999). These strategies are further discussed, and examples of how to apply them in an instructional environment are included in Table 5.3.

Table 5.3 Examples to incorporate strategies within phase 2: reflection-in-action

Create a learning environment to enhance reflection-in-action	• Include authentic activities • Expose learners to a variety of experiences • Provide learners' autonomy • Extend the learning experience over an appropriate length of time • Incorporate multiple forms of reflection before, during, and after the experience
Create an environment that allows for social interaction with others to promote reflection-in-action	• Observe peers in practice • Observe experts in practice • Collaborate in groups
Engage in informal mindfulness exercises to promote reflection-in-action	• Be mindful while engaging in all activities • Focus attention within the environment • Maintain a personal awareness
Provide feedback	• Instructor identifies strengths and weaknesses • Students ask questions throughout the experience • Provide results of performance from peers and instructor

5.3.1 Create a Learning Environment to Enhance Reflection-in-Action

There are several environmental variables that can be included to enhance reflection-in-action during situated learning. Creating an authentic experience is the heart of situated learning and provides the foundation on which the theory is based. Authentic learning environments are those in which learners are provided contexts and activities utilizing knowledge as it would be applied in real-life situations outside of a traditional classroom environment (Herrington and Oliver 2000). In regard to reflection, when learners are able to identify and connect to an authentic activity, the quality and level of reflection is enhanced. Additionally, the longer the situated learning experience, the greater involvement and engagement the student has with many of the challenges and issues faced within practice. Therefore, learners acquire the ability to reflect spontaneously and independently within the situation.

5.3.2 Provide Social Interaction with Others

Social interaction is also key in facilitating R-I-A. While reflection is often considered a personal introspective activity, within situated learning, it is very much a social process. When learners interact with peers in activities, R-I-A is facilitated as they develop their own personal awareness through comparison and critical analysis of their actions, allowing for adjustments in the present moment. Social interaction can occur through many ways, as listed in Table 5.3, such as through peer observation, group work, and group discussion during the experience. Also, interacting and engaging in self-comparison to expert performance facilitate immediate reflection, helping learners to adjust to surprises through innovative and interactive methods.

5.3.3   Engage in Informal Mindfulness Exercises

Mindfulness practices will vary based on the purpose and environment in which one is practicing. R-I-A occurs as one is engaged in an activity or experience. Therefore, to enhance R-I-A, one needs to engage in mindfulness during this activity. Informal mindfulness, or being mindful during everyday activities, creates a space that allows learners to attend to themselves, the surrounding environment, and to the present moment. Directing attention through informal mindfulness helps the learner process the situation and better attend to necessary details, prevents overburdening cognitive load, and helps the learner adjust through R-I-A. Several informal mindfulness strategies can be incorporated during the experience to promote R-I-A among the learners. When mindfulness strategies are incorporated into a situated learning environment that includes the above design considerations, an ideal instructional environment is created for R-I-A and promoting reflective practitioners.

Informal mindfulness practices, as developed in the mindfulness orientation and over the course of the experience, should be coupled with engaging in R-I-A for learners to experience the optimal learning benefits. This includes being mindful as they observe, interact, and participate in the activities of the learning environment. Examples of incorporating informal mindfulness are included in Table 5.3.

5.3.4   Provide Feedback

The final element designers should include to enhance R-I-A during the learning experience is feedback. Feedback strategies that have been shown to enhance reflection in situated learning include the instructor or expert providing real-time feedback by identifying strengths and areas of improvement, the opportunity for students to ask questions throughout the situation, and the students receiving the results of their performance from their peers and instructor immediately. Evidence within the literature indicates that when incorporating mindfulness strategies to support R-I-A during the learning situation, these feedback strategies help the students see the value in reflection (Stalmeijer et al. 2009) and provide support to students when struggling with difficult situations (Herrington et al. 2014). Feedback provides immediate information that helps one R-I-A (Seibert 1999) and identify alternative procedures and perspectives, exposing areas in need of improvement (Jordan 2010).

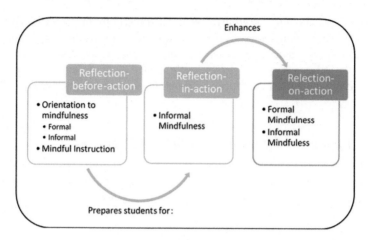

Fig. 5.4 A conceptual model of reflection in situated learning highlighting reflection-on-action

5.4   Reflection-on-Action

R-O-A is an important design element for reflection in situated learning (Fig. 5.4). Most models and frameworks of reflection in situated learning have focused on R-O-A. Students should have the opportunity to reevaluate the situation and, through the reflective process, will begin to integrate new knowledge for future use (Herrington and Oliver 2000). As multiple forms of reflection are important to the reflective process, R-O-A provides an additional means to develop reflective practitioners. R-O-A allows the student to process and critically analyze new information and strategies gained from the learning experience (Seibert 1999). Depending on the learning environment, R-O-A can be accomplished in many ways including, but not limited to, journaling, group discussion, blogging, and, if possible, nonlinear navigation or the ability to return to sections of the experience through methods such as reviewing recorded observations or working backward through previous sections of a computer-mediated module.

Reflection-on-action is directly related to mindfulness practices and enhanced by R-I-A. Practitioners, or in this case students, who learn to effectively reflect-in-action and critically reflect-on-action, have the ability to improve their tacit knowledge and further improve everyday performance. When learners engage in R-I-A supported by mindfulness, they are able to find more meaning in the present moment, which, in turn, enhances the meaning-making process when they engage in R-O-A (Horton-Deutsch et al. 2012). Additionally, as included in the first two phases of this model, mindfulness strategies should be included in the R-O-A phase (Table 5.4). For R-O-A, formal mindfulness practice is appropriate as it creates a cognitive space that allows the learner to direct all attention to the moment of thinking and processing the previous learning experience. Formal mindfulness will assist the learner in centering his or her thoughts and feelings on one specific event or topic to prevent outside distractions within and outside of the cognitive space.

Table 5.4 Examples to incorporate strategies within phase 3: reflection-on-action

Provide the opportunity for learners to reflect on the practice	• Journaling • Group discussion • Returning to sections of the experience through reviewing recorded observations or nonlinear navigation
Learners engage in formal mindfulness	• Mindfulness of sound or "listening out" to help reflect on work in relation to a broader perspective • Breath-focused mindful attention, mindful listening • Sitting meditation • Body scan

Formal mindfulness practices can be used to bring the learner to the present moment, reducing distraction and focusing attention. Through informal practices, while reflecting on the learning experience, they will have stronger attention and metacognitive abilities to evaluate their thoughts, perceptions, and outcomes in order to reassess and improve future performance.

References

Anglin, L. P., Pirson, M., & Langer, E. (2008). Mindful learning: A moderator of gender differences in mathematics performance. *Journal of Adult Development, 15*(3), 132–139. https://doi.org/10.1007/s10804-008-9043-x.

Bell, A., & Mladenovic, R. (2015). Situated learning, reflective practice and conceptual expansion: Effective peer observation for tutor development. *Teaching in Higher Education, 20*(1), 24–36. https://doi.org/10.1080/13562517.2014.945163.

Birnbaum, L. (2008). The use of mindfulness training to create an 'accompanying place' for social work students. *Social Work Education, 27*(8), 837–852. https://doi.org/10.1080/02615470701538330.

Bohecker, L., Wathen, C., Wells, P., Salazar, B. M., & Vereen, L. G. (2014). Mindfully educating our future: The MESG curriculum for training emergent counselors. *The Journal for Specialists in Group Work, 39*(3), 257–273. https://doi.org/10.1080/01933922.2014.919046.

Boudreau, J. D., Macdonald, M. E., & Steinert, Y. (2014). Affirming professional identities through an apprenticeship: Insights from a four-year longitudinal case study. *Academic Medicine, 89*(7), 1038–1045. https://doi.org/10.1097/ACM.0000000000000293.

Bush, M. (2011). Mindfulness in higher education. *Contemporary Buddhism, 12*(1), 183–197. https://doi.org/10.1080/14639947.2011.564838.

Carmody, J., & Baer, R. A. (2008). Relationships between mindfulness practice and levels of mindfulness, medical and psychological symptoms and well-being in a mindfulness-based stress reduction program. *Journal of Behavioral Medicine, 31*(1), 23–33. https://doi.org/10.1007/s10865-007-9130-7.

Carroll, M. (2009). From mindless to mindful practice: On learning reflection in supervision. *Psychotherapy in Australia, 15*(4), 38.

Croker, F., Alison, J., Stillman, G., White, B., & Tonkin, C. (1998). Situated learning as a model for the design of an interactive multimedia program on medication administration for nurses. *Innovations in Education & Training International, 35*(4), 329–336. https://doi.org/10.1080/1355800980350408.

Crumley, G., & Schutz, H. (2011). *Short-duration mindfulness training with adult learners* (Vol. 22, pp. 37–42). Bowie: American Association for Adult and Continuing Education.

Diaz, F. M. (2011). Mindfulness, attention, and flow during music listening: An empirical investigation. *Psychology of Music, 41*(1), 42–58. https://doi.org/10.1177/0305735611415144.

Edwards, P. M. (2010). Theories-in-use and reflection-in-action: Core principles for LIS education. *Journal of Education for Library and Information Science, 51*(1), 18–29.

Eick, C. J., Ware, F. N., & Williams, P. G. (2003). Coteaching in a science methods course: A situated learning model of becoming a teacher. *Journal of Teacher Education, 54*(1), 74–85. https://doi.org/10.1177/0022487102238659.

Eyler, J. (2001). Creating your reflection map. *New Directions for Higher Education, 2001*(114), 35–43. https://doi.org/10.1002/he.11.

Goh, E. (2012). Integrating mindfulness and reflection in the teaching and learning of listening skills for undergraduate social work students in Singapore. *Social Work Education, 31*(5), 587–518. https://doi.org/10.1080/02615479.2011.579094.

Granville, S., & Dison, L. (2005). Thinking about thinking: Integrating self-reflection into an academic literacy course. *Journal of English for Academic Purposes, 4*(2), 99–118. https://doi.org/10.1016/j.jeap.2004.07.009.

Herrington, J., & Oliver, R. (2000). An instructional design framework for authentic learning environments. *Educational Technology Research and Development, 48*(3), 23–48. https://doi.org/10.1007/BF02319856.

Herrington, J., Parker, J., & Boase-Jelinek, D. (2014). Connected authentic learning: Reflection and intentional learning. *Australian Journal of Education, 58*(1), 23–35. https://doi.org/10.1177/0004944113517830.

Horton-Deutsch, S., Drew, B. L., & Beck-Coon, K. (2012). Mindful learners. In *Reflective practice transforming education and improving outcomes* (pp. 79–96). Indianapolis: Sigma Theta Tau International Honor Society of Nursing.

Huisman, S., & Edwards, A. (2011). Experiential learning: An exploration of situated and service learning. *AILACTE Journal, 8*, 15.

Jordan, S. (2010). Learning to be surprised: How to foster reflective practice in a high-reliability context. *Management Learning, 41*(4), 390–412. https://doi.org/10.1177/1350507609357388.

Keevers, L., & Treleaven, L. (2011). Organizing practices of reflection: A practice-based study. *Management Learning, 42*(5), 505–520. https://doi.org/10.1177/1350507610391592.

Langer, E. J. (2000). Mindful learning. *Current Directions in Psychological Science, 9*(6), 220–223. https://doi.org/10.1111/1467-8721.00099.

Langer, E. J., & Piper, A. I. (1987). The prevention of mindlessness. *Journal of Personality and Social Psychology, 53*(2), 280–287. https://doi.org/10.1037//0022-3514.53.2.280.

Langer, E. J., Hatem, M., Joss, J., & Howell, M. (1989). Conditional teaching and mindful learning. *Creativity Research Journal, 2*(3), 139–150. https://doi.org/10.1080/10400418909534311.

Mapel, T. (2012). Mindfulness and education: Students' experience of learning mindfulness in a tertiary classroom. *New Zealand Journal of Educational Studies, 47*(1), 19.

Mishna, F., & Bogo, M. (2007). Reflective practice in contemporary social work classrooms. *Journal of Social Work Education, 43*(3), 529–544.

Ovens, A., & Tinning, R. (2009). Reflection as situated practice: A memory-work study of lived experience in teacher education. *Teaching and Teacher Education, 25*(8), 1125–1131. https://doi.org/10.1016/j.tate.2009.03.013.

Pezzolesi, C., Ghaleb, M., Kostrzewski, A., & Dhillon, S. (2013). Is mindful reflective practice the way forward to reduce medication errors? *International Journal of Pharmacy Practice, 21*(6), 413–416. https://doi.org/10.1111/ijpp.12031.

Richey, R. (1986). *The theoretical and conceptual basis of instructional design* (Vol. Book, Whole). New York/London: Kogan Page.

Richey, R. (2005). Validating instructional design and dvelopment models. In *Innovations in instructional technology: Essays in honor of M. David Merrill* (pp. 171–185, Vol. Book, Whole). Mahwah: L. Erlbaum Associates.

Ritchhart, R., & Perkins, D. N. (2000). Life in the mindful classroom: Nurturing the disposition of mindfulness. *Journal of Social Issues, 56*(1), 27–47.

Russell, A., Norton, C. L., Uriarte, J., & Wisner, B. (2011). Reflective teaching in social work education: Findings from a participatory action research study. *Social Work Education, 30*(4), 392–407. https://doi.org/10.1080/02615479.2010.500658.

Ryu, J., & Lee, D.-m. (2015). Mindful learning in geography: Cultivating balanced attitudes toward regions. *Journal of Geography, 114*(5), 197–210. https://doi.org/10.1080/00221341.2 015.1046897.

Seibert, K. W. (1999). Reflection-in-action: Tools for cultivating on-the-job learning conditions. *Organizational Dynamics, 27*(3), 54–65. https://doi.org/10.1016/S0090-2616(99)90021-9.

Shapiro, S. L. (2009). *The art and science of mindfulness: Integrating mindfulness into psychology and the helping professions* (Vol. Book, Whole). Washington D.C.: American Psychological Association.

Song, K. Y., & Muschert, G. W. (2014). Opening the contemplative mind in the sociology classroom. *Humanity and Society, 38*(3), 314–338. https://doi.org/10.1177/0160597614537794.

Spiro, R. J., Coulson, R.L., Daniel, A.K. (1988). Cognitive flexibility theory: Advanced knowledge acquisition in ill-structured domains. Technical Report No. 441. University at Illinois at Urbana-Champaign. Champain, IL.

Stalmeijer, R. E., Dolmans, D., Wolfhagen, I., & Scherpbier, A. (2009). Cognitive apprenticeship in clinical practice: Can it stimulate learning in the opinion of students? *Advances in Health Sciences Education, 14*(4), 535–546. https://doi.org/10.1007/s10459-008-9136-0.

Stewart, T. (2010). Opening up service-learning reflection by turning inward: Developing mindful learneres through contemplation. In *Problematizing service-learning critical reflections for development and action* (pp. 37–70). Charlotte: Information Age Publishing.

Trunnell, E. P. (1996). Optimizing an outdoor experience for experiential learning by decreasing boredom through mindfulness training. *The Journal of Experimental Education, 19*(1), 43.

Chapter 6
Conclusion and Future Direction

Situated learning, reflection-in-action, and mindfulness are three distinct fields that are brought together in this monograph to illustrate how learners in a situated learning environment can engage in mindful practice to enhance their ability to reflect-in-action and overall reflective practice. Expanding on theorists' work in experiential learning and sociocultural theory, the theory of situated cognition and situated learning evolved, grounded in the idea that learning and cognition are dependent upon the context in which they are embedded (Herrington and Oliver 2000; Brown et al. 1989). In a situated learning environment, learners participate in authentic tasks, often through means of apprenticeships, anchored instruction, or computer-mediated simulations. Designing instruction for situated learning can be difficult as authentic environments are often unpredictable and vary greatly across situations and disciplines (Winn 1993). To support situated learners in facing these ill-structured problems and unique environments, it has been suggested that it is essential to develop skills that transfer across environments (Winn 1993). By integrating strategies to promote reflective practice and mindfulness in the design of situated learning environments, instructional designers can use this model to address many of the challenges faced in the variable and uncertain environments that arise within situated learning.

The conceptual model presented in this monograph was developed through synthesizing theories and methods from three different areas of study, providing a new perspective and instructional approach for designers. Mindfulness is one area of study many are not familiar with, especially the impact it can have within an educational environment. If learners are able to direct their attention to the present moment by practicing mindfulness, it is likely they will be able to engage in the critical thinking processes involved in reflection. Reflection-in-action is another area that has yet to be strongly considered as making an impact within situated learning. Therefore, by incorporating mindfulness and reflection-in-action within situated learning, this conceptual model presents an approach that has potential to improve reflection and positively impact outcomes in situated learning.

© Association for Educational Communications and Technology 2018
A.M. Stoner, K.S. Cennamo, *Enhancing Reflection within Situated Learning*,
SpringerBriefs in Educational Communications and Technology,
https://doi.org/10.1007/978-3-319-70326-8_6

This monograph summarizes how mindfulness can be beneficial for learning outcomes within an educational environment. Within the model, it emphasizes the potential for promoting reflection-in-action and improving performance. While this model was built based on addressing an instructional issue within situated learning, the concepts and relationships within the model are thought to have the potential be generalizable beyond situated learning. Reflection-in-action and mindfulness are essential skills that can be translated across instructional environments; however, further studies will need to be conducted in order to confirm these patterns. Exploring these concepts and relationships in other areas of educational research will be extremely beneficial in continuing the exploration of mindfulness to enhance reflective practice within education.

This model was developed and is provided to help provide a foundation not only for designers but also for future research. Design and development research is often an iterative process of development and evaluation for continual improvement (Richey and Klein 2007). Therefore, future research studies should implement and test this model within an actual situated learning environment. Testing the model will allow for further formative evaluation and also provide guidance for the development of a procedural model that will help designers work through a step-by-step process in designing reflection activities that incorporate mindfulness for situated learning. As an initial step in this process, it is hoped that the model and strategies identified herein will be of use to both practitioners and researchers who wish to explore mindfulness as a means of enhancing student reflection strategies within situated learning and other instructional environments as well.

References

Brown, J. S., Collins, A., & Duguid, P. (1989). Situated cognition and the culture of learning. *Educational Researcher, 18*(1), 32–42. https://doi.org/10.2307/1176008.

Herrington, J., & Oliver, R. (2000). An instructional design framework for authentic learning environments. *Educational Technology Research and Development, 48*(3), 23–48. https://doi.org/10.1007/BF02319856.

Richey, R., & Klein, J. D. (2007). *Design and development research: Methods, strategies, and issues* (Vol. Book, Whole). Mahwah: L. Erlbaum Associates.

Winn, W. (1993). Instructional design and situated learning: Paradox or partnership? *Educational Technology, 33*(3), 16.

Appendix A. Teaching Mindfulness Resources for Educators

1. Mental Fitness Inc. includes a 5 min mindfulness curriculum with videos, guided scripts, and handouts and resources for a classroom environment.

   http://mentalfitnessinc.org/index.php/5-minute-mindfulness/

2. Mindful Teachers: Living, Learning, and Teaching with Mindful Awareness: This is a blog created by a teacher who incorporates mindfulness in her teaching. She provides information on mindfulness along with mindfulness training links, activities, and teaching resources for all levels.

   http://www.mindfulteachers.org/p/free-resources-and-lesson-plans.html

3. McCown, D., Reibel, D., & Micozzi, M. S. (2010). *Teaching mindfulness: a practical guide for clinicians and educators* (1. Aufl.;1; ed.). New York; London: Springer.

   This is a practical guide to mindfulness for both teachers and clinicians. It describes mindfulness in a clear and easy-to-read manner, along with providing resources for mindfulness and vignettes of mindfulness-based interventions from actual classes.

4. Mindful Schools provides courses, resources, and curricula for integrating mindfulness in K-12 educational environments. They have a large focus on schools with students facing high stress and high turnover rates. This website provides resources for both teachers and students.

   http://www.mindfulschools.org/

5. Mindful – Taking time for what matters. Getting Started with Mindfulness: Mindful is both a magazine and website where one can find information and guides to incorporating mindfulness across any environment. The Getting Started with

© Association for Educational Communications and Technology 2018
A.M. Stoner, K.S. Cennamo, *Enhancing Reflection within Situated Learning*,
SpringerBriefs in Educational Communications and Technology,
https://doi.org/10.1007/978-3-319-70326-8

Mindfulness is a great introduction to helping a beginner answer questions, understand the basics, and even practice with a guided 5 min mindfulness exercise.

https://www.mindful.org/meditation/mindfulness-getting-started/

Index

© Association for Educational Communications and Technology 2018
A.M. Stoner, K.S. Cennamo, *Enhancing Reflection within Situated Learning*,
SpringerBriefs in Educational Communications and Technology,
https://doi.org/10.1007/978-3-319-70326-8

Printed by Printforce, the Netherlands